To Byron Kadadwa

A METHUEN PAPERBACK

First published as a Methuen Paperback original in 1984 by
Methuen London Ltd, 11 New Fetter Lane, London EC4P 4EE
and Methuen Inc, 733 Third Avenue, New York, NY 10017.

British Library Cataloguing in Publication Data

Soyinka, Wole
   A play of giants.
   I. Title
   822   PR9387.9.S6

   ISBN 0-413-55290-X

Set in IBM 10 point Journal by 🄰 Tek-Art, Croydon, Surrey
Printed in England by Whitstable Litho Ltd, Whitstable, Kent

Wole Soyinka

A PLAY OF GIANTS

METHUEN · LONDON AND NEW YORK

CHARACTERS

BENEFACIO GUNEMA
EMPEROR KASCO
FIELD-MARSHAL KAMINI
GENERAL BARRA TUBOUM
African heads of state

GUDRUM, *a Scandinavian journalist*
CHAIRMAN OF THE BUGARA CENTRAL BANK
SCULPTOR
BUGARAN AMBASSADOR
MAYOR OF HYACOMBE
PROFESSOR BATEY
TWO RUSSIAN DELEGATES
TWO AMERICAN DELEGATES
TASK FORCE SPECIALS
GUARDS
SECRETARY-GENERAL OF THE UNITED NATIONS

The action takes place at the Bugaran Embassy to the United Nations, New York. The time is a few years before the present.

On the Heroes of our Time: some personal notes

No serious effort is made here to hide the identities of the real-life actors who have served as models for *A Play of Giants*. They are none other than: President for Life Macias Nguema (late) of Equitorial Guinea; Emperor for Life (ex) Jean-Baptiste Bokassa of the Central African Republic; Life President Mobutu Sese Koko etc, of Congo Kinshasa (just hanging on); and — the HERO OF HEROES in the person of Life President (ex) the Field-Marshal El-Haji Dr Idi Amin of Uganda, DSc, DSO, VC etc, etc, who still dreams, according to latest reports, of being recalled to be the Saviour of Uganda once again.

It is obvious that no single play should even attempt to contain such a gallery of Supermen. I therefore shift the blame for this act of hubris to Jean Genet (*The Balcony*) who suggested the idea, that is, provided a model of form which might possibly attempt the feat. Naturally I absolve Genet of the short-comings in execution.

Unlike many commentators on power and politics, I do not know how monsters come to be, only that they are, and in defiance of place, time and pundits. According to some of these last, our grotesqueries are the product of specific socio-economic histories, yet no one has ever satisfactorily explained why near-identical socio-economic conditions (including a similar colonial experience) should produce on the one hand, a Julius Nyerere and on the other, an Idi Amin. What we are able to observe more confidently (in addition to their mechanisms for first acquiring power) is how our subjects succeed in remaining entrenched in power long after they have been unambiguously exposed for what they are. Mobutu, to take our surviving example, should have received his *coup de grace* at least a decade ago but for the resolute interests of the Western powers — Belgium, France and West Germany most directly.

Such a seemingly straight-forward identification of interests fails to apply however when we come to the figure of Idi Amin. This certified psychopath was sustained in power at various periods by group interests and ideologies as varied as those of Great Britain (which installed him in power in the first place), the United States, the Soviet Union, the Organisation of African Unity, Cuba, Libya, the PLO and Israel, not to mention the vociferous support accorded him by the cheer-leaders among the intelligentsia of the African continent and the Black Caucuses of the United States.

That genuine ignorance accounted for part of this phenomenon is not to be denied. As Secretary-General of the Union of Writers of the African Peoples and the editor of a journal both of which organs were mobilised to confront the tyranny of Amin's regime, I did however have the opportunity of engaging, at first hand, politicians, intellectuals and even Heads of State in the effort to expose the truth about Uganda under Idi Amin. My experience in the majority of cases was that such ignorance was willed, not fortuitous. The tone, the varied disguises of their 'ignorance' left me with the confirmation of a long held suspicion that power calls to power, that the brutality of power (its most strident self-manifestation) evokes a conspiratorial craving for the phenomenon of 'success' which cuts across all human occupations. This may be one of the many explanations why some of the most brilliant men of science and the humanities bend their skills and intelligence to ensuring the continuity of power even in its most brutal, humanly exhorbitant manifestation. (Hitler, Stalin are our notorious examples). It certainly makes it easier to understand why some of our own colleagues, including those of the Left, could find it possible to rationalise and applaud the crudest barbarities of an Idi Amin — their 'success' is reflected and consumated in the Colossal Success which Amin's power symbolised, even in its very excesses!

Pinochet, Galtieri, Pol Pot (who will have us believe he is now reformed and a patriot to boot), d'Aubuisson and his Right-wing murder squads, confidently striving for the ultimate legitimation of his innate propensities . . . all masters of the statecraft of 'disappearance' whose magnitude acts inversely to magnify their own appearance. Yes, we do know what is at stake, what is being fought over. The puzzle which persists is why some, but not others actually enjoy, indeed *relish* the condition of power, why certain individuals would rather preside over a necropolis than not preside at all, why, like the monkey in the folk tale, some would rather hold on to the booty of power through the gourd's narrow neck than unclench the fist and save themselves.

Power, we have suggested, calls to power, and vicarious power (that is, the sort enjoyed by the politically impotent intelligentsia) responds obsequiously to the real thing. Apart from self-identification with success, there is also a professed love (in essence a self-love) which is perverse, being also identical with the 'love' of the slave-girl for her master. Often, on listening to the rationalisations of this group, I feel that I am listening to a slave-girl in a harem, excusing the latest sadisms of the seraglio, exaggerating the scattered moments of generosity, of 'goodness', forgetting that even the exceptions to the rule merely emphasise the slave relations between herself and the Master. Our friends professed to find in Idi Amin the figure of a misunderstood nationalist, revolutionary and even economic genius — after all, he did boot out the blood-sucking Asians, and was he not always to be relied on for a hilarious insult against one super-power imperialist chieftain or another and their client leaders on the continent? And so the Organisation of African Unity remained deaf to all objections and proceeded to honour him with the chairmanship of that body, an honour later denied Colonel Ghadafi, his erstwhile protector when it came to that maverick's turn. That irony would not have been lost on the Ugandan survivors of Amin's reign of terror, but I doubt if many of them shed any tears over the injustice.

In human terms, what happened in Uganda was this: that nation lost its cream of professionals, its productive elite. That much is no longer denied, the pitiful list of the notable 'desaparecidos' is no longer disputed except by the deaf and the blind. But Uganda also lost tens of thousands of faceless, anonymous producers, workers and peasants who were ghoulishly destroyed by this mindless terror; the attendant economic disaster is still with Uganda, compounding her political instability. Even more sobering is the continuing horror of daily existence, the brutalisation of normal sensibilities which is apparent in the conduct of the ongoing resistance to Milton Obote's rule and in the government's pattern of repression on sections of the populace. What is being claimed here, in effect, is that the longer a people are subjected to the brutality of power, the longer, in geometric proportion, is the process of recovery and re-humanisation.

Byron Kadadwa to whom this play is dedicated is representative of the many thousands whose contribution to the nation of their birth was brutally cut short by Idi Amin. He led his theatre troupe to the Festival of Black and African Arts (FESTAC) in Nigeria, 1977. Shortly after his return to Kampala, he was arrested — for reasons which are ultimately unimportant, dragged from rehearsals by the notorious State Research Bureau and later found murdered. His successor, Dan Kintu met a similar fate, together with playwright John Male. The relations of all three had to pay substantial bribes to the police before their bodies were even released for burial. Need one add the footnote that, following these warnings, the rest of the troupe fled into neighbouring countries?

Now why does one say that the 'reasons' for Byron Kadadwa's arrest are ultimately of no importance? That the reasons why any one of the missing thousands came to the 'notice' of Idi Amin at all did not really matter? Only because this was the reality, as testified to by Ugandans themselves, including one of the most notable survivors, the late Robert Serumaga. Robert was, to start with, one of the most ardent supporters of Idi Amin. It is no exaggeration to say that he actually prospered under his regime. Shortly after Amin's seizure of power, we met in a European capital where we café-crawled one night till nearly dawn, while he bombarded me with arguments, (buttressed by Ministry of Information tracts) in favour of the coup. I was equally adamant in my negative view which was based on my knowledge of Idi Amin's history as a cold-blooded killer and my partiality (then) to Milton Obote who appeared to be embracing the socialist creed just before the coup. Serumaga's faith in Idi Amin was based on a genuine assessment, by him, of Idi Amin's leadership qualities and what he saw as a relaxing of constraints on individual liberty imposed by Obote. The 'excesses' which, even then, were already gaining publicity, he defended as genuine accidents which Idi Amin himself regretted and deplored. Over-enthusiastic subordinates were, in Serumaga's view, mostly to blame.

Robert Serumaga was then a member of the editorial board of *Ch'Indaba* (former *Transition*), whose editorship I had recently assumed. So convinced was I of what Robert refused to accept that I took the precaution, not merely of removing him from the editorial board, but of writing him a formal letter to that effect. I quoted his glowing statements of support for Idi Amin, commenting that these were incompatible with *Ch'Indaba's* editorial position, and wished him luck.

My next meeting with Serumaga took place about two years later at Victoria Station where he had gone to see off his theatre company on their way to Gatwick Airport and home. They were just returning from a tour of the Soviet Union. I plunged straight into the apology which I had rehearsed for our next face-to-face encounter, explaining the brusqueness of my letter as a deliberate insurance for his own life which I knew would be endangered, sooner or later, like all others. Robert cut me short by confirming the worst.

He was convinced that the letter had indeed enabled him to survive. It had been intercepted and, first the Head of Amin's Security Service, then Idi Amin himself summoned him to discuss its contents. Our Hero even tried to persuade Robert to try and recover his position on the journal where he could keep an eye (and perhaps some control) on our activities which, I was informed by the then Head of Ghanaian Security, had already come to the attention of Idi Amin. (He had sent a protest through his ambassador about the Union's use of Ghana as a base for 'subversive' activities against his government.) Serumaga said, 'I told him, sir, but you see what is in the letter. The man has sacked me; he didn't simply ask for my resignation, I've been given the boot.' The incident assisted Robert in remaining secure in Idi Amin's trust for a long while, compared to others who never even served on the Editorial Board of *Ch'Indaba* or contributed to its activities. But inevitably, even Robert discovered that he was living on borrowed time. He was seeing off his troupe but had decided to remain behind to look for an apartment in London. Then a quick trip home to evacuate his wife, family and immediate dependants, after which — self-exile. Robert's explanation for this reluctant decision was simple but chilling; it has not been possible for me to forget the very words he used:

'At the start,' he said, 'you more or less knew what to do and what to avoid if you wanted to stay alive. You knew when to speak, when to shut up and what to say or not say. Now there are no longer any rules. What saved you yesterday turns out to be your death-warrant today. I have no friends, no colleagues left. They are all dead, or escaped. But mostly dead.'

Robert Serumaga later joined the Liberation movement against Idi Amin, broadcasting from Tanzania during the struggle. Those same intellectuals we have spoken of began to raise the academic issues of the role of the Tanzanian Army in that war. They had found Idi Amin's prior bombings of incursion into Tanzanian territory, boastfully publicised in the familiar Arminian cacophony, mainly amusing, certainly no worse than 'naughty'. But now Tanzania mobilised itself, counter-attacked, and those same cheer-leaders suddenly recalled issues of 'territorial integrity', 'external interference' etc, etc, as the Tanzanian Army, motivated in the way Idi Amin's could never be, swept the latter aside in a record time for any military disintegration in recent times.

Robert Serumaga died of illness. He had at least the satisfaction of participating in the successful end to a repellent dictatorship. I do not know if, were he still alive today, he would consider Uganda truly liberated — that is a question which a Ugandan playwright will, I hope, be moved to tackle before long. For now . . . (*Enter brass band, Ring Master, up platforms, hoops, and trampolines*) . . . 'Ladies and Gentlemen, we present . . . a parade of miracle men . . . (*Cracks whip.*) . . . Giants, Dwarfs, Zombies, the Incredible Anthropophagi, the Original Genus Survivanticus, (alive and well in defiance of all scientific explanations) . . . ladies, and gentlemen . . .'

Wole Soyinka

PART ONE

Three figures are seated in heavy throne-like chairs at the top of a wide, sweeping stone stairway. Behind them runs a curving gallery, with framed portraits, really the balcony of the upper floor, windows overlooking a park, across which is a skyscraper, the UN building, in silhouette. The balcony railing is opulently gold-gilt. One of the figures, a huge man (KAMINI) is in military dress uniform, its massive frontage covered in medals. On one side of him is a comparatively dwarfish creature (KASCO) who appears to be a deliberate parody of the big man. His costume is the same, down to the last medal. In addition, however, he wears a cloak of imperial purple. Flanking the central figure on the other side is a tall, thin man (GUNEMA) in tails of immaculate cut. His own decorations consist simply of a red sash and blue rosette, plus a medal or two.

GUDRUM, a stout, florid and rather repulsive Nordic type sits half-way up the steps, gazing in obvious adoration at KAMINI. From time to time she inspects the SCULPTOR's labour.

The ground floor is a lounge which has been turned into a studio. A SCULPTOR is working at a life-size group sculpture of the three 'crowned heads', on which any likeness is hardly yet apparent. When the sitters speak, they do so stiffly, in an effort to retain their poses. But first the tableau is revealed in silence, the SCULPTOR adding putty here and there or scraping away.

GUNEMA. Ah, *el poder, amigos,* to seek the truth of the matter, these subversives, *guerilleros,* they do not really seek to rule, no, not to administer a space, not to govern a *pueblo, comprendo?* No, mostly they seek power. Simply power.

KASCO. But that is obvious, no? It is not the lust for responsibility which makes the social misfits to become guerrillas.
If you think first of responsibility and governing, you give up
search for power. Lust for power, *oui*. But lust for
responsibility — I never hear of it.

GUNEMA. Ah, but I have not finished. Beyond *la responsabili-
dad*, beyond politics lies — ah — power. When politics has
become routine, organised, we who are gifted naturally with
leadership, after a while, we cease to govern, to lead: we
exist, I think, in a rare space which is — power.
Es verdad, no?

KAMINI. Only one thing to do to subversive — khrr! (*A
meaningful gesture across his throat.*) I used to have
subversives too. The Western Press like to call them guerrillas.
I say, I have no guerrillas in my country. Only bandits. We
call them *kondo*. I catch any *kondo*, I make him smell his
mother's cunt.

GUDRUM. I know all about subversives. My over-permissive
country is full of them, hiding from their failure to cope
with reality. Unfortunately we Scandinavians still take a
spurious pride in our so-called liberal ideas, open our doors
to all sorts of ne'er-do-wells from the Third World who
ought to be in their countries, contributing something to
development. As a journalist I get to meet many of them.
Effete youngsters who hang around the cafés and wine-bars
and disco joints, useless to themselves and to their nation.

KAMINI. Gudrum very good friend of African leaders. She
writing book about me with many photographs. She calling
it, *The Black Giant at Play*. It show Kamini very very jovial
family man. Big uncle to everybody in country.

GUDRUM. It would be finished by now if I didn't have to take
time dealing with the slander spread by those Bugaran
runaways in my country. They spread the most disgusting
libel against the Field-Marshal. They are pouffes, most of
them. Faggots.

GUNEMA. What mean pouffes? Or faggots.

GUDRUM. Cissy. Homosexuals. They don't know what it is to be a man. They are terrified of virility.

KAMINI (*laughing*). Gudrum, I think you tell me, they even run away from real woman. Like you.

GUDRUM. Of course Your Excellency. They have become part of the culture of drug dependency. A continent of the future, which Africa is, does not need their type. They would only contaminate its soul, its history. You have your heroes, Excellency, nation-builders. Today, we are lucky to have in you their reincarnation. Those statues my Life President — a very brilliant idea. It will serve to prick the conscience of the United Nations.

KAMINI. You very good lady Gudrum. Just remember to give names of these subversives. Even if they refuse to come home, we find their villages. Only one treatment good for family which support guerrillas hiding in Scandinavia and other American-type countries.

GUNEMA. *Si.* For my country also. But sometimes I look at country like Italy. Red Brigade. Or Germany. Or these new people, the Armenian Brigade who assassinate and bomb airport no matter where. I do not think they seek government. Because why? Because they already enjoy power. Secret power. They strike, hold hostage, bomb office, kill person they do not know before, total stranger — is that kind of power I talk about. I think that kind, he only seek to redress history, not take government. But he enjoy secret power.

KAMINI. All subversives bad people. Mostly imperialist agents. Better you kill them first.

GUNEMA. Of course, of course. Very definitely. I am not sentimental, no.

KASCO. Sentiment? No. Was Saint-Just sentimental?

KAMINI. Saint-Just? Who was Saint-Just?

KASCO. Executioner of the French Revolution. He take care of Danton — guillotine. Saint-Just was a soul-brother to the immortal Robespierre. But they all make mistake. Too many people drink this power. Every riff-raff from *poubelle* — the sans-cullottes, Girondists, Jacobins, Montagnards, bakers, tavern-keepers even forgers and convicts. Opportunists. That is what destroy Robespierre. Power was debased. Power is indivisible.

GUNEMA. Is why I like voodoo. That also secret power. *Mysterioso, pero amigo, tambien — muy peligroso.* For those who are not chosen, very dangerous. Is not suddenly that it manifest itself, like Red Brigades. All of them very sudden, like ejaculation. Voodoo power is tranquil, *extendido,* like you making love to woman you really love or possess. You dominate her but still you make the love prolong, not to body alone but to her soul.

KAMINI. Ah, now I understand. Before you talk like all those my Bugara professors. When they want to think subversive, they talk in that way to make confusion. But the woman matter, oh yes, Kamini in full agreement. That is why is good a leader should have many wives.

The door opens gently and a face peeks round.

CHAIRMAN. May I come in Your Excellency?

KAMINI. Who? Ah come in, come in. Why you take so long Mr Chairman? (*He turns to his companions.*) You excuse me while I talk some business. Is my chairman of Bugara Central Bank. When I travel, I take Bank of Bugara with me, then nobody can steal money behind Kamini's back. Too many *kondo* wearing European coat and tie and forging signature of this and that bank manager. When Kamini not home, only chairman can sign cheque, and he here with Kamini. (*He guffaws.*)

KASCO. *C'est sage, mon vieux.*

KAMINI. So what happen? How much loan they give us?

CHAIRMAN. Your Excellency, it was a difficult meeting. The World Bank was not very cooperative.

KAMINI. They don't give loan?

CHAIRMAN. Not exactly, Your Excellency. They simply insisted on certain conditions . . .

KAMINI. What I care about conditions? Agree to any conditions just get the loan.

CHAIRMAN. It is not quite as easy as all that Your Excellency. They want to mortgage Bugara body and soul . . .

KAMINI. I say what I care about body and soul? If they can loan Bugara the two hundred million dollars, I give them body and soul. Go back and agree to any condition they want.

CHAIRMAN. There is more to it, Your Excellency. They don't even want to hand over the money directly. In fact, the Board dismissed that request outright. There was no discussion.

KAMINI. What they mean by that? You not tell them Bank of Bugara is here with President in person?

CHAIRMAN. Your Excellency may rest assured that I explained the position very thoroughly. But their decision is that they would only fund specific projects with the loan.

KAMINI (*flaring up*). So they can come and send their stinking spies into Bugara saying they come to supervise loan project? No deal. Kamini wise to their game of infiltrating Third World country with their syphilitic spies. Go back and tell them either they loan ready cash direct, or I take over all remaining foreign business in Bugara. Any member country of World Bank with business in Bugara, we nationalise.

CHAIRMAN. Your Excellency, I did outline that possibility to them. I left them in no uncertainty of such a consequence.

KAMINI. And still they say no?

CHAIRMAN. I'm afraid so Excellency. (KAMINI *falls silent, chewing his lips*.)

GUDRUM. It's a plot my Life President. It is part of their deliberate economic sabotage.

KAMINI. I know. Is dirty capitalist plot all over. World Bank belong to everybody. Why they are discriminating against

Bugara alone? Why they give Hazena loan? You tell me
Hazena still owe them more money than Bugara, not so?

CHAIRMAN. That is a fact Your Excellency. I pointed it out to
them.

KAMINI. Aha! So what they say? What they say to that enh?

CHAIRMAN. They replied that Hazena had been paying interest
regularly Your Excellency.

KAMINI (*angrily*). What I care about rotten interest? Bugara
promised to pay everything all at once, in five years. So what
I care about stupid interest enh? Taking interest and taking
interest and finishing up all Bugara foreign exchange.

GUDRUM. Bugara has more than contributed its quota to the
World Bank, that is a fact, Your Excellency. When the
economy was buoyant Bugara never missed a payment.

KAMINI. Is what am saying and is all discrimination and dirty
imperialist plot. I make complaint to Secretary-General
today and raise matter in General Assembly. Let World
Bank tell us once for all if it is just for rich countries and
neo-colonial bastards like Hazena or it belong to Third
World countries who need loan. As for you, get back to
Bugara right away and start printing more Bugara bank notes.
I show the bastards at least they can't control Bugara
sovereign currency.

CHAIRMAN (*aghast*). I beg your pardon Dr Life President?

KAMINI. I said go back and get cracking with government mint.
When I return I want to see brand-new currency notes in
circulation, not hearing all this grumble of shortage of money
and so on and so forth.

CHAIRMAN. But Your Excellency, that's why we came to seek
this loan in the first place. Now that we haven't got it, there
is nothing to back the new currency with.

KAMINI. What the man talking about? You short of good
currency paper at government mint?

CHAIRMAN. I'm trying to explain, Your Excellency. Even
now, at this moment, our national currency is not worth

its size in toilet paper. If we now go ahead and print more, it would . . .

KAMINI. What? What you say just now?

CHAIRMAN. Your Excellency?

KAMINI. I say, what you talking just now about Bugara currency?

CHAIRMAN. Just that all currency needs backing Your Excellency. It must be . . .

KAMINI. No, you said Bugara currency only worth something this and that.

CHAIRMAN. Oh. I was trying to explain that any paper money is only worth what . . . (*He trails off.*)

KAMINI (*rising*). You saying Bugara currency only worth shit paper? Is that what I hear you say just now? Is that what I hear you say just now?

CHAIRMAN. Your Excellency, I was only trying to illustrate . . .

KAMINI (*to* KASCO *and* GUNEMA). You see, is this kind of traitor I have in charge of Bugara Central Bank. This syphilitic bastard talking worse than imperialist propaganda.

CHAIRMAN. Your Excellency . . .

KAMINI. Is no wonder Bugara getting broke all the time, when this kind of chairman insulting Bugara national currency, calling it shit paper to everybody. This the kind of person going to important meeting of World Bank to ask for loan. You think World Bank give Bugara loan when you calling national currency shit paper?

CHAIRMAN (*falling on his knees*). My Life President, I assure Your Excellency I never . . .

KAMINI. Today I make you eat good old Bugara shit. (*He reaches for the bell.*)

CHAIRMAN (*abject with terror*). Your Excellency, my Life President . . .

KAMINI. Taking around with me sneaking traitors left and right talking bad about Bugara. Today I make you smell your mother's cunt . . .

Enter a TASK FORCE SPECIAL.

TF SPECIAL. Your Excellency?

KAMINI. Take this coat-and-tie *kondo* inside that toilet room there and put his head inside bowl. (TF SPECIAL *proceeds upstairs.*) Each time the tank full, you flush it again over his head.

TF SPECIAL *hauls up the pleading* CHAIRMAN *by the shoulders and shoves him towards a door leading from the balcony.* KAMINI *follows, he stands just outside the doorway giving instructions as the* CHAIRMAN, *struggling, is forced to his knees.*

Push his head deep inside. I say deep inside. Put your bloody foot on his neck and press it down. (*Sounds of gurgling.*) That's better. Now pull chain. (*Noise of rushing water follows.* KAMINI *beams broadly.*) Good. Call Bugara currency shit money, not so? So you drink some shit water for now until Kamini ready for you. (*Returning to his seat.*) You leave door open so I can hear water flushing his stinking mouth.

From now on until towards the end of the play, the sound of the emptying cistern will be heard, periodically. KAMINI *resumes his seat. He turns to his companions.*

I'm sorry my brothers. I hope you excuse that little interruption while I taking care of business.

KASCO. *Mais pas de quoi, mon frère.*

GUNEMA. *Si, comprendido.* Discipline must be imposed.

KAMINI. Is no wonder he fail to get the loan. He already go there with bad attitude of mind to subvert Bugara economy. Now if I go and complain that World Bank refuse Bugara loan, they will just tell me, your chairman of Central Bank already admit your currency is shit money and so on and so forth.

GUDRUM. We could send the Minister of Finance next, my Life President.

KAMINI. Yes, but I wait now until my statue goes up in the United Nations. When everybody see it standing there I think it give the World Bank something to think about. Is they who will come this time and beg me to talk business all over again.

The AMBASSADOR *enters, opening the door with the greatest deference and speaking almost apologetically.*

AMBASSADOR. Your Gracious Excellency, I think I have found the right spot to display the sculpture.

KAMINI. Yes?

AMBASSADOR. I think not only Your Gracious Excellency, but your comrade Presidents, their Excellencies will be pleased. The position is not too dissimilar to this present one. It is the top of the stairs dominating the passage which all delegates must pass through on leaving the General Assembly for the Committee and public reception rooms. Visitors who come to consult the delegates cannot fail to see your Excellencies' commanding figures.

KAMINI *turns to his companions one after the other.* KASCO *responds with a wide grin of approval and a nod.* GUNEMA *slightly inclines his head.* KAMINI *resumes his pose.*

KAMINI. My brothers approve. See that the Secretary-General is informed. The protocol officer will see me to arrange the unveiling ceremony. Gudrum, you will give him advice? I think you have informed the World Press.

GUDRUM. Of course Dr President. I am looking forward to the historic moment. In fact, maybe I ought to go and inspect the location myself.

KAMINI. Very good idea. Go with Ambassador and bring me report.

The AMBASSADOR *bows and leaves, accompanied by* GUDRUM. *Again a brief period of silence as the* SCULPTOR

*continues his work, the trio having resumed their stiff
postures.*

I like the Secretary-General. He's a nice man.

KASCO *grins and nods.*

GUNEMA. *Si. Pero,* him *niño.* Baby. No, him like child,
pequeño. Not understand power. Not use power. Good man,
si, muy simpatico pero, not man of power.

KAMINI. It is good like that. He is to carry out our orders. We
come here to give him orders. We have the power, not him.

KASCO. *Oui, oui. Le pouvoir, c'est a nous.*

KAMINI. What?

KASCO. Power, is we. We have ze power.

KAMINI. Is good like that.

Some moments silence. Suddenly GUNEMA *sighs.*

GUNEMA. Sometimes I dream . . . *El caudillo.*

The others turn to him puzzled.

El Caudillo, General Franco. Yes, Franco I think he make
better Secretary-General. Is good for world peace. Spain very
peaceful for forty years. Now everybody make trouble.

KAMINI. Franco? Was he not friend of Zionists?

GUNEMA. *El caudillo?* No no no. If General Franco Secretary-
General, first he finish off the Zionists.

KAMINI *nods approval.*

KASCO. What you think of Papa? I think he makes good
Secretaire-General.

GUNEMA. Papa Doc? Papa Doc Duvalier? Si, he is man of
power but er . . .

KASCO. No, Papa de Gaulle, the saviour of modern France. He
was like a Papa to my people. I wept when he died.

GUNEMA. I think first you meant the strong man of Haiti.
Now that was *un hombre!* The power! *Misterioso.* He was
Franco of the Caribbean. But I don't think he make good
Secretario, oh no!

KAMINI. Why?

GUNEMA. Voodoo. Too much voodoo. It give him power, plenty power. He will put voodoo over all the delegates and make them zombie.

KAMINI. Even you my brother? Oh you are making joke. Everybody knows you are a man of voodoo yourself.

GUNEMA. Not like Papa Doc. He was *maestro. El uno, y unico*. He turn nearly half of Haiti into zombie and the rest — (*He makes a slashing gesture across his throat.*) he send his Ton Ton Macoutes. Even the Ton Ton are zombie. Papa Doc can give them order from anywhere. He can be one end of island and *think* to them — do this or do that. And they do it. Distance no importance. Now that is power. But too much for *Secretario. Muy peligroso.*

KAMINI. You think Papa Doc can put voodoo on somebody like me?

GUNEMA. Impossible! *Jamas,* never! My friend, you are not *un hombre ordinario.* Like me and our *camarade* the Emperor Kasco, we are not *ordinario.* Why you think we rule our people? Some people are born to power. Others are — cattle. They need ring in their nose for us to lead.

KASCO. *Oui oui.* There are persons, individuals who are born with the imperial sign here (*He taps his forehead.*) on head. Me, I think — de Gaulle. Robespierre. But the prime, the leader of them all in history, in all the world history — the *sans pareil* of all time is Napoleon Bonaparte!

GUNEMA. No, is Franco.

KASCO. Franco is like midget in history when you compare with Bonaparte. Franco! Franco was — he did not even have a presence. No command in personality.

GUNEMA. Is Franco, is Franco. You do not know history, you only know French.

KASCO. My friend, to know French is to understand history. In Napoleon Bonaparte you have the entire history of modern Europe and its civilisation . . . even North Africa entered history with Napoleon.

KAMINI. My brothers, what are we fighting about? What about our very own brother, Chaka? For me, Chaka is greatest. Only Hitler can compare to Chaka. Even then, if Chaka had aeroplanes and flying bomb, he would have conquered Hitler. I know, because I am descended from the great Chaka.

KASCO and GUNEMA turn to look at him, then at each other. KASCO gives an embarrassed cough while GUNEMA lifts a cynical eyebrow.

GUNEMA. Of course *amigo*. If you are not descended from the great Zulu, who is?

KAMINI. The history department of my university trace my family tree for me. They announce it in the newspapers and give lecture on television. It make my people very happy.

KASCO. *Naturellement!*

KAMINI. Even our lives are very similar. I too, I kill my first lion at seven years old, with a spear. It is part of our tradition. The test of manhood. At thirteen years, the young boy must go into the bush, all by himself. He takes a spear and a *panga* — cutlass you know — and he lives in the bush until he can come home with a kill. For other people it is always a small antelope, or a baby water-buck. Me, after five days, I track down a lion and kill it.

KASCO. But my brother, you said you did this at seven years!

KAMINI. Yes, at seven. Others thirteen, but me, I could not wait. Like Chaka, I could not wait.

The door begins to open, very gingerly. Again the AMBASSADOR's head appears, this time naked fear showing on her face. She looks steadfastly at KAMINI, then withdraws without shutting the door. Seconds pass, then the door is pushed firmly open. GUDRUM enters first, then beckons and more or less drags in the AMBASSADOR. She musters some measure of resignation which does not disguise the very real terror beneath. She coughs to attract KAMINI's attention.

AMBASSADOR. Your Gracious Excellency . . .

KAMINI. What is it? Why do you continue to disturb?

AMBASSADOR. They've gone, Your Excellency. The rest of the delegation, they've gone.

KAMINI *sits bolt upright, grasping the arms of the chair.*

KAMINI. What did you say?

GUDRUM. Some more traitors have shown their true faces, Your Excellency.

AMBASSADOR. They left straight after the working session of the Foreign Ministers' Committee. The Foreign Affairs Minister, his secretary, the two specialists on the Palestinian and South African problems — Dr Wamue and Mrs Olanga, and that new . . .

KAMINI. My speech! What happen to speech he prepare for me to address General Assembly tomorrow. He suppose to read it to me over lunch.

AMBASSADOR. I shall assign it immediately to the Third Secretary, your Gracious Excellency.

KAMINI. The Third Secretary. The Third Secretary to write address of Bugara's Life President which he make to United Nations?

GUDRUM. Actually he is very bright, Dr President. A young graduate but very bright.

KAMINI. The Third Secretary! You, Madame Ambassador, you have been mistake in appointment. Why can you not write the address? Why? Because you are ignorant! If I have no expert why are you ambassador if you are not expert? Why can you not represent my opinion and put it correctly if I am not here.

GUDRUM. Of couse she can Your Excellency. I could lend a hand too if Your Excellency wishes. But this young graduate has studied all the Life President's speeches at the university. He did his doctorate on the very subject. I have read some of the briefings he prepared for the delegation.

KAMINI (*relaxing somewhat*). Is that so? I know that my

political philosophy and so on are studied in the university but I did not know that somebody has been getting doctorate degree from them. Did he get this doctorate from our own Bugara University?

AMBASSADOR (*eagerly*). Certainly Your Excellency. And he has given many public lectures on the subject since he took up position here.

KAMINI. Very good, very good. But where is the First Secretary?

AMBASSADOR. That position has been vacant for two years Your Excellency, same thing for the Second Secretary. If Your Excellency will be kind enough to recall the several memos I sent to the Minister of Foreign Affairs on the subject, copied to Your Excellency. . .

KAMINI. All right. What is the young man's name?

AMBASSADOR. Seli Metatu, Your Excellency.

KAMINI. Promote him First Secretary and tell him to get on with my speech. Still, I don't like idea of Third Secretary writing speech for a Life President. Promote him today.

AMBASSADOR. But, if er . . . if I may make bold to remind Your Excellency, the reason why the post of First and Second Secretaries, plus that of Commercial Attaché have been vacant is that, well, according to the Foreign Affairs Minister, there are no funds to pay anyone in those grades.

KAMINI (*screams*). I remember very well. I do not forget. And is that not the same minister who has now run away in the middle of his international mission? Why did he run away? Why do they all run away? Because they steal Bugara money, that's why. They smuggle goods and do black market, ruining Bugara currency! You tell me, why that traitor, the one who calls himself professor, why he run away instead of leading my team of delegation to this meeting here? He embezzle money and he suspect that Kamini find out. He know I want to disgrace him before his international friends at the United Nation Assembly — a common thief like that. With all his grey hairs he is so shameless. So everybody thinking

him a great scholarship man, a brilliant man and so on and
so forth. A brilliant man to be embezzling money and
running away. Thank you very much for brilliance, I take
stupid man any day. I promote that young man, today. When
he come back to Bugara, see that he go to university and
make him professor. But if he try to be brilliant like Kiwawa,
he will smell his mother's cunt before he can run away. Now
I find new Foreign Minister who will find money and pay
salaries instead of running away with Bugara money. Perhaps
I make you the Foreign Minister, you are useless as
ambassador when you cannot write my speech in emergency.

AMBASSADOR. Your Gracious Excellency's orders will be
carried out.

KAMINI. How did they get away? I want the names of my
Task Force Specials who are watching their movement hand
and foot. How did all of them escape without being
followed? I tell them to watch carefully even when they go
toilet to shit.

AMBASSADOR. I have already set up an enquiry Your
Excellency. They must have planned it very carefully. They
pretended they were still holding their meeting in the
committee room but in fact they had all escaped through the
lavatory window. It opened into a passage used only by the
cleaners in the building. The Presidential Task Force guards
kept waiting at the door for over an hour before . . .

KAMINI. What fools! Did they not notice that they can no
longer hear anything? Did they think the delegation was
sleeping or what?

AMBASSADOR. Your Gracious Excellency, they were clever.
They left on a tape recorder of conversations which must
have kept running for an hour or more.

KAMINI. You see. Is it not a disgrace? A whole minister of
state, he is playing tricks like 007 James Bond in order to
run away with national funds. That is the kind of ministers
left in Bugara. James Bond. That is what result from
imperialism and neo-colonialism and the culture they teach
our people. Syphilitic culture. Mental syphilis. How you

explain a thing like this? An educated man, a cabinet minister playing like James Bond in the United Nations.

AMBASSADOR. Your Excellency, if I may . . .

KAMINI. Don't interrupt. You are not a good ambassador or this would not happen under your nose. Have you telexed Bugara for the Task Force to go to these people's villages?

AMBASSADOR. Your Gracious Excellency, I was about to suggest that I run over to a friendly embassy and use their telex.

KAMINI. Why a friendly embassy? Why not our own telex?

AMBASSADOR. It was cut off months ago, Your Excellency. We . . . could not pay . . . we had no funds to settle our bills. (*Speaking more hurriedly*.) The Foreign Minister was aware of . . .

KAMINI. The Foreign Minister! I do not want to hear the name of those traitors — any of them. Just get a message any way you like to my Presidential Task Force Specials and dispatch them to their villages. You have already lost precious time Madame Ambassador. And report the matter to the Secretary-General of the United Nations. Let him know what bad things his people have done to me.

AMBASSADOR. I will attend to it Your Excellency. (*She hurries out followed by* GUDRUM.)

KASCO. *Mes condolences, camarade.* But these are the tiny thorns that trouble the head of crown.

GUNEMA. *Si. Que lastima.* But, it is nothing. Traitors breed like maggots, no? They are rotten to the bone, to the tissue inside the bone. Their souls fester with corruption. They infect others.

KASCO. I see you send to the village. That is good. The root may have poisoned the surrounding soil.

GUNEMA. My subjects, they are very careful how they plot against Benefacio Gunema. When I look at each one of my ministers, or army officer, he knows I am looking into the heart, into the very soul of his village. He know that I see through his head into the head of his wife, his children, his father and mother and grandfather and uncles and all his dependents, all his kith and kin, living or dead . . . yes, including the dead ones. It is he who must choose whether they lie in peace in their graves because, *la culpabilidad,* the — er — guilt, it extends beyond the grave.

KAMINI (*still agitated*). I think it is difficult now to sit and pose for artist. We take a break now and fill the stomach a bit, what do you say?

KASCO. *Oui, d'accord.*

GUNEMA. Agree. My bottom of spine is beginning to feel mighty cramp.

KAMINI. Good. My good friend Mr Sculptor, we take break now. You too, I think, you take break. All work and no play . . . not so? When my ambassador lady comes, you tell her I say she give you taxi money because I like you.

SCULPTOR. Oh there will be no need for that Your Excellency. I get paid all my expenses.

KAMINI. What is the matter? You don't like me? You don't take my money?

SCULPTOR (*hurriedly*). No Your Excellency, on the contrary . . .

KAMINI. Maybe you don't like American dollars. Bugara money good enough for you? (*He takes out thick wads of notes and thrusts them at the* SCULPTOR.) There. Good Bugaran currency.

SCULPTOR. Mr President sir . . .

KAMINI. Dr President.

SCULPTOR. Your Excellency, Dr President is most generous.

The door is flung wide open by the AMBASSADOR *who ushers in a* VISITOR.

AMBASSADOR. Your Excellencies, His Excellency the Life President of Nbangi-Guela.

Enter LIFE PRESIDENT BARRA TUBOUM. *He is dressed in a striped animal skin 'Mao' outfit with matching fez-style hat. He sports an ornately carved ebony walking stick. At his waist is strapped an ivory-handled side-arm stuck in a holster which is also made of zebra skin.* KAMINI *rushes at him, arms outstretched. The other two follow more slowly.*

KAMINI. Alexander! Welcome, welcome.

TUBOUM *stops short, seems to recoil.*

TUBOUM. Tuboum, my brother, Barra Tuboum.

KAMINI. Barra Tuboum?

TUBOUM. Barra Boum Boum Tuboum Gbazo Tse Tse Khoro diDzo. I have abandoned all foreign names.

KAMINI. My brother, I congratulate you.

They embrace.

TUBOUM. You did not hear about it? I have begun a vigorous campaign to eliminate all foreign influences from our people. I took the lead and changed my own names. Even the names of my father's headstones, I changed. All names on our cemeteries will be changed.

The others applaud mildly and embrace, French-style.

GUNEMA. Alexander was an African. You must study your history. It has been proved conclusively that he was African.

KASCO. But surely the name . . .

GUNEMA. African to the core. But, it does not matter. The rebellion is what I want to hear about. Is it finish?

TUBOUM. You see me here, do you not? Of course it is finished. Crushed. All the ring leaders? — Tsch! (*He makes expressive gesture.*) Except three. I brought them with me to exhibit before the General Assembly. They have confessed that some foreign powers were behind the rebellion. After public confession, perhaps we serve them up at cocktail party.

GUNEMA. *Hijos de puta!*

KASCO. Imperialist swine!

KAMINI (*leads with the general back-slapping*). I congratulate you my brother. I congratulate you again.

KASCO. Bravo! You have served good lesson on our enemies.

GUNEMA. I still wish you do not change name. After this, everybody will have call you Alexander the Great. Who will remember name of Barra Tuboum?

TUBOUM. Oh yes they will. After this victory it is a name no one will ever forget. I led my forces in person, the famed striped leopards of Mbangi-Gwela.

GUNEMA. Ah yes, *amigo*, I always mean to ask, a striped leopard, is a real animal? It really exists?

TUBOUM. A chimera perhaps. A phantom, a sphinx. But it is a fearsome part of our lore, a mystery creature which stalks at night. Nobody sees it and returns to tell the tale. Yet the tale is there, terrifying. My elite troops must be fearless and mysterious. Do they exist? They appear. They complete their task, they vanish — back to their camp at Lake Gwanza. They do not mix with the populace. In action they eat with their leader, the only being whose orders they understand. They know they are the elite, they bathe in the same ambiance of power, terribly invincible. They train in secret, far from the prying eyes of the common herd. Their secrecy is their power, like the hair of Samson; the eyes of any stranger at the mysteries of their self-preparation is a corrosion of that power. They kill such strangers, and they eat them.

KASCO. Eat them!

TUBOUM. Eat them — white, black or yellow. Is it not the only way to ensure the re-absorption of that power of yourself which has been sucked away by profaning eyes? Oh they are as fearsome as they are fearless, my striped leopards of Gwanza. The rebels were desperate too, the tribe of Shabira, mean, cruel, unscrupulous. What is the Geneva Convention to them? They took hostages, workers at the mines of Shabira, their families, priests, nuns, children, foreigners and citizens alike. Our allies the French paratroops arrived. What to do about the hostages? Nothing. The Belgian commander had no qualms — the eggs must be broken before the omelette. Rebellion is a cancer, worse than death, worse than rape or mutilation. Rebellion is an enemy of growth. Better the loss of a few children than the poisoning of their growth by the horror of rebellion. The Belgians asked no questions, they took orders and filled in the gaps. My leopards were mean and taut. I propelled them like a fine-honed shaft along River Butelewa. We swept down on the rebel stronghold at dawn; they were sated from plunder and rape but for all that, fierce and savage. The hostages? What does a violated nun hope for? Many fell before our own bullets, the rebels had turned coward, hiding behind the very habits they had defiled. We moved from street to street, from square to square. They retreated. We followed. They moved into their last redoubt, a fortified hill, riddled with bunkers, oh, they had been a long time preparing this rebellion. In their confusion they no longer could be certain who was friend or foe. We pin-pointed them by their own voice: *'Qui va la?'* a voice would cry, and my canons responded: 'Boom, Boom Tuboum'. *'Qui va la?'* again and again. 'Boom, Boom Tuboum. Boom, Boom Tuboum.' Till at last, covered in masonry and blood, they began the surrender.

KAMINI. Ah yes? You take many prisoners?

TUBOUM. Only a handful, enough for the celebration feast of my striped leopards. The rest, had they not committed murder and rape? We did not even give them a soldier's death. We hanged them, and left them hanging.

One by one they go up to TUBOUM, *embrace him and kiss him formally on both cheeks.*

KASCO. *C'est vraiement heroique. Félicitations!*

GUNEMA. I envy you *amigo*. A brave man, a leader of enormous courage.

KAMINI (*grips him by the shoulders*). As you speak, I wish I am there by your side. A man comes to life, in middle of battle, not so? He feel power beating through his blood, like madness.

GUNEMA. I envy you three, *amigos*. Warriors. You take power
through army. You fight. You conquer. It is different for
me. I feel like odd man out. Power is something I must
experience another way, a very different way. Your method
is straightforward, it has a clarity, *muy hermoso,*
mathematical. I inhabit, I think, the nebulous geography of
power. That is why, always, I am searching to taste it. You
understand, really taste it on my tongue. To seize it *a la
boca,* roll and roll it in the mouth and let if trickle inwards,
like an infusion. Once, only once, I think I succeed.

KASCO. Courage does not come only in war, *mon ami*. In
matter of courage, it is clear you are *pareil* with all of us. I
fight for the French wars in Indo-China, but on the
battlefield, an enemy is just an enemy. We fight, we kill,
or we die. I have been thinking, what you say before, I agree
with you. Power comes only with the death of politics. That
is why I choose to become emperor. I place myself beyond
politics. At the moment of my coronation, I signal to the
world that I transcend the intrigues and mundaneness of
politics. Now I inhabit only the pure realm of power. I fear,
mes amis, all three of you have chosen to remain in the
territory of politics. But — is it choice? Or are you trapped?

KAMINI (KAMINI *shakes his head in bewilderment*). Lunch my
brothers, lunch! Are we hungry or not?

The door is flung open again and the AMBASSADOR
announces:

AMBASSADOR. Your Excellencies, the Honourable Mayor of
Hyacombe and his party!

Preceded by a beadle (PROFESSOR BATEY) *who carries a
golden key on a red velvet cushion, the* MAYOR *enters in
full regalia, chain and all. He makes a low bow, sweeping the
floor with his hat, and suddenly freezes. He comes up very
slowly, his eyes popping.* GUDRUM *squeezes her way past them.*

MAYOR. Your Gracious Excellency, we did not know that you
had guests. I mean . . . and such guests. Your Excellencies!
The entire continent of Africa is here!

KAMINI. My friend Mr Mayor, these are my brothers. They are not guests.

MAYOR. So His Excellency General Barra Tuboum was able to visit us after all. The media said there were some problems . . .

GUNEMA. Imperialist conspiracy. He crush it — boom boom. Like Alexander the Great.

KASCO. No. Like Napoleon!

MAYOR. Your Excellencies, you will have to excuse me. I feel rather embarrassed. You see, we did not expect to meet . . . I mean, we only have one key.

TUBOUM (*looking round in puzzlement*). Key? What key?

MAYOR. The key to the city of Hyacombe Your Excellency. We had made an appointment with President Dr Kamini to make a presentation today. Freedom of the city of Hyacombe. Now we find four of you. My heart is bursting. All leaders who have given us our pride of race. You who have uplifted us from the degradation of centuries of conquest, slavery and dehumanisation. Your Excellencies, the city of Hyacombe will never forgive me if I fail to maximise this unique occasion. All four Excellencies must be presented with the freedom of the city. We shall make this an annual public holiday in Hyacombe.

BATEY (*tugs him by the sleeve*). Mr Mayor . . .

MAYOR. Yes? Oh, do forgive me Your Excellencies. I should have begun by introducing my delegation. This is Professor Batey, one of our councillors, in charge of protocol. He is of course our link with his Excellency Dr Kamini.

KAMINI. Of course I know my good friend professor. (*He hugs him, to* BATEY's *physical discomfort.*) Come and meet my brothers. My brothers, this is Professor Batey, very good friend. He is writing book on me which he call *The Black Giant at Work*. You know Gudrum is doing the other one, *The Giant at Play*. People think Big Uncle Kamini never play, but Miss Gudrum will show them. This is President-for-Life Signor Gunema of . . .

BATEY. Let me save you the trouble Your Excellency, I know everyone of their Excellencies, although I have not had the honour until now. Sirs, I cannot tell you . . . I am overwhelmed. I mean, all at once. When we tell them back in Hyacombe, no not just Hyacombe, when the entire nation gets to know this, that we were able, at one and the same time to shake hands with . . . I mean, to stand within the same four walls in the presence of . . . please, forgive me, I am a very emotional person . . . (*He turns away, whipping out his handkerchief.*)

KAMINI (*turning to his guests*). Professor Batey is like that, a very kind person. When he visited me in Bugara too, he cried, just like that. And you know why he cried? Because of all the bad propaganda which the imperialist press was making against me. They said I killed people, that I tortured people and lock them in prison — all sorts of bad things about me because I, Life President Dr Kamini, I tell them to go to hell. No black man ever tell them like that before.

BATEY. You did sir. You told them the way we like to hear it here.

KAMINI. Professor Batey, he come, he see with his own eyes. He travel throughout the country and he not see any single person being killed, not one person being tortured. He return to his country and he write nice things which he has seen with his own eyes.

BATEY (*recovered*). Your Excellency, it was my duty as a scholar to present the truth. The problems of Bugara were purely economic — as a sociologist, I saw that only too clearly. Bugara has not only inherited a discredited economic system from its colonial history, she is still being exploited by a neo-colonial conspiracy of multi-national conglomerates which continue to prey on developing countries in the Third World. It is an outrageous and inhuman situation Your Excellencies, and I hope you lay it on them again when you address the General Assembly tomorrow. What sickens one most of all is the hypocrites who raise the diversionary scarecrow of human rights when in this very country . . .

MAYOR. Professor . . . Professor Batey . . .

BATEY. What?

MAYOR. We have an immediate problem.

BATEY. I beg your pardon.

MAYOR. That's all right. It's all in your address, so save it.
Your Excellencies, I have thought up a solution — if you will
be so kind as to indulge us. We must fix a new appointment.
Give us time to get more keys. And Professor Batey of course
will have to include all Your Excellencies in his address.

GUDRUM. With your permission, Your Excellency, just what I
was going to suggest. We must use the occasion to make
history. The embassy will fix a new time which gives us time
to invite the Press and television.

KAMINI (*turns to his colleagues*). Does this meet with your
approval my brothers? (*They chorus 'Si, si', 'D'accord' etc.*)
We are all agreed Mr Mayor. Everything, we like to do
together. Like statues there. I insist we present united,
collective front in all matters. We show these super powers.

MAYOR. It is an inspiring example Your Excellency.

KAMINI. Goodbye my friend. Oh, perhaps while you are here,
you can help me look at the speech which I am making in
the General Assembly tomorrow. My ambassador will show
you a copy. It had to be written by one of the junior
secretaries in our embassy and I have not yet tested him
properly.

BATEY. A junior secretary? What about my friend Dr Kiwawa?
I was looking forward to seeing him here — at the head of
your delegation as usual.

KAMINI. Dr Kiwawa, he turn bad. He disappeared the very
day we ready to travel here for the Assembly. In fact three
of my team of advisers disappeared with him. They run
away after they embezzle money from the Treasury. My
police could not find them till now, perhaps they have run
to the neighbouring country.

BATEY. Dr Kiwawa! But that is incredible Your Excellency!

I thought I knew him so well. Oh, but this is most discouraging, Dr President.

KAMINI. And then since we arrive here, five more have disappeared from United Nations. I know they have been bribed to run away by capitalist money. Soon they will start to write bad things about me in the capitalist press when the truth is that they ran away from guilty conscience. I know they were in this embezzlement plot with Dr Kiwawa.

BATEY (*firmly*). You must contact Interpol Your Excellency. I regret that I ever placed such reliance on him.

KAMINI. I have sent to inform the Secretary-General. After all, I come here on the affairs of the United Nations. I want him to know what bad things the imperialists are doing to me just because I champion the cause of our people.

BATEY. It is sad Your Excellency, very sad. I shall certainly lend a hand with your delegation while you are here, sir. It is an honour. I gratefully accept.

KAMINI. My friend, I cannot thank you enough. Goodbye Mr Mayor.

The Mayoral delegation leaves, ushered out by the AMBASSADOR. GUNEMA *shakes his head.*

GUNEMA. Nobody on my delegation will ever run away.

KAMINI. Anybody can run away.

GUNEMA. No. Not my delegation. And you know why?

KASCO. You keep them happy with women?

GUNEMA. No. Voodoo. They know if they desert on duty, something bad will happen to them. They will fall sick with horrible disease. They will die very slowly.

TUBOUM. Yes, the whole of Africa knows of your reputation in that direction. Does it work all the time?

GUNEMA. You had better believe it.

TUBOUM. It is simpler just to take their family hostage. At home, anyone who gets sent on an official mission leaves his family behind, under strict surveillance.

KAMINI. I do that too. But sometimes they bribe the guards and smuggle out the families. There is so much corruption. One man cannot supervise everything.

GUNEMA. You can, with voodoo. From here I am surveillancing everything at home. Every one of my subjects, I see. The ones who are plotting, who think they can overthrow Benefacio Gunema, I see them. And the plots of my super-cillious aristocracy, the mestizos, I see. They think they superior to Benefacio because I, I am full negroid, and I arise from low background, poor environment — I see them. Fools! They do not understand yet that some am born to rule. It is there, in the signs since I am born. I am different being from everybody else. I wipe my feet on their necks, mestizos, aristocrats and conspirating negritos alike. (*His eyes become progressively hard, staring into the distance*.) Power is the greatest voodoo and voodoo is greatest power. I see, I surveillance all of my subjects — wherever I am. Nobody stage coup d'etat for Gunema and live to tell the story. No public servant steal money from Benefacio and nobody run away when I send him on important mission.

KASCO. Never?

GUNEMA. Never. It never happen. Even my political prisoners I see when they begin to plan escape from prison.

TUBOUM. Lucky for you. You've only got a small island, easily patrolled by a canoe or two with outboard motors. Do you know the sheer size of Mbangi-Gwela? Even I don't know half of what is inside it.

GUNEMA. Size is not important. I know everything.

KASCO. Well, I have no problems of escapees. We are French. My government people are proud to be French, all my officials. To try to escape from la France — *mon Dieu* — who ever heard of such a thing?

KAMINI. My brothers, let us go and eat. It is long past time for food. We continue our discussion of politics over a good dinner, not so?

KASCO. *Ah oui. Moi, j'ai faim.*

As they leave, the SCULPTOR *stares after them in exasperation. He flings down his implements and begins to take off his overalls.* GUDRUM *has remained behind.*

GUDRUM. When will your work be completed? That is, tomorrow what time?

SCULPTOR. Tomorrow what time? Are you being funny? May I just remind Your Excellency that when I came here, it was only to sculpt the President and the President only. No one said anything about the other two. They were never even considered back at headquarters — I mean, I have no doubt that they are very important in their own country, probably more important, but they don't make quite the same splash on world headlines as your President Kamini.

GUDRUM. His Gracious President invited the others. It's a brilliant fraternal gesture.

SCULPTOR. Fraternal gesture? Very good. I am not arguing. My bosses are not arguing, I mean, they agreed to it didn't they? But don't come and expect me to perform miracles when a single sculpture suddenly becomes a family portrait. An extended family portrait — if you'll excuse the racial joke.

GUDRUM. It must be completed tomorrow, that is our understanding. The discussions I held with your bosses in London made that quite clear. Their Excellencies are unveiling the work jointly before the closure of the ongoing session of the General Assembly — that's the day after tomorrow.

SCULPTOR. Did you tell them that in London? As far as I recall, you only told them that you would like it exhibited at the UN before it goes over to London for our own exhibition.

GUDRUM. Your own exhibition?

SCULPTOR. Hey, what's the matter with you? Madame Tussaud's waxworks exhibition. That's what brought me here in the first place, isn't that right?

GUDRUM. Oh that. That has been overtaken by events; I should have thought that was obvious.

SCULPTOR. Obvious my God! Not obvious to me it isn't. And certainly not obvious to them in London. Madame Tussaud's want to open their new Africa section — it's part of our anniversary celebrations. That's why we made contact with the embassy. *We* made the contact, remember?

GUDRUM. I shall speak again to your London office. You've got it all wrong.

SCULPTOR. No, you've got it all wrong. And let me tell you something else, if their Excellencies keep bobbing up and down the way they've been doing all this week, and adding more and more Excellencies to the group, I will never get it finished, not even for our own exhibition. I may as well pack it all up and go home for all the good I'm doing here.

GUDRUM. Please get this into your head. First, that sculpture is going on permanent exhibition in the United Nations. Next, you had better get it ready so we can move it there latest tomorrow night.

SCULPTOR. Are you giving me orders? Christ, you don't even know the first thing about this sort of thing do you? You don't exhibit any damned sculpture in this state, not with this stuff you don't. This is just the model. At Madame Tussaud's, we make a wax mould of it and that is what we exhibit. We are a waxworks museum. Strictly between you and me, this one should go into the Chamber of Horrors — that's where it belongs. Personal opinion, that's all. But if you want to exhibit it permanently at the United Nations I expect you'll be wanting it cast in bronze or something. So one way or the other, this object here can't stay as it is in no damned United Nations.

GUDRUM. I see. So it is your opinion that His Excellency belongs in the Chamber of Horrors?

SCULPTOR. Hey, you are not offended are you? Oh come on . . . what are you anyway? His mistress? What does he do to you eh?

Without a change of expression, GUDRUM *storms out of the room.*

SCULPTOR (*his laughter dies abruptly*). Oh my god, I hope she doesn't go and report to the Ambassador. Or even to the Life President himself. (*He shrugs.*) To hell with that. They won't dare sack me till I finish the job. Ah well, better keep this moist. No knowing when we get to start again.

He begins to cover the sculpture in plastic. The door opens slightly but no one enters for some moments. Then KAMINI's *bulk slowly pushes its way in.*

KAMINI (*beaming broadly*). Ah my good friend, how's the work going?

SCULPTOR (*startled*). Oh I didn't hear you come in. Er . . . to be honest your Excellency, this thing doesn't look like it will be ready on time.

KAMINI. But why not? You are very good worker. I like you.

SCULPTOR. Well, now that you ask me your Excellency, I shall try to explain something about this job. It is not always clear to laymen you see.

KAMINI. Explain? Explain what?

SCULPTOR. It's about this commission you see, sir. For one thing, that lady — not the Ambassador, the white one, she was just telling me it must be ready tomorrow.

KAMINI. Oh I am sure. You are a good worker. I watch you. Some time you come to my country. I invite you. You meet other artists like yourself. Traditional. European. The lot. You ever see a Makongo carving?

SCULPTOR. I can't say I have, Your Excellency. I am really not an artist as such. I just copy the original so to speak.

KAMINI. Nonsense. You great artist. I like you. Tell that Ambassador to remind me, I invite you to Bugara. You and our Makongo carvers, you exchange ideas. I know they will like you. When they see how their President like you, they will like you like a member of the family. You will become one of the family. Perhaps you even marry one of our girls eh?

Good for world peace I always say. I like inter-marriage between all races.

SCULPTOR. I shall be honoured to visit Mr President.

KAMINI. Dr President, Field Marshal El-Hajj Dr Kamini, Life President of Bugara.

SCULPTOR. I beg your pardon, Dr President. As I was saying sir, I shall be very honoured.

KAMINI. You like, I promise you. So, you hurry up and finish work and you come as my special guest. Right, you finish tomorrow.

SCULPTOR. Dr President sir, Your Excellency, there is something I have to explain. I mean, you just don't understand!

KAMINI (KAMINI *freezes*). You say what?

SCULPTOR. I know how it is, I mean, I don't expect a layman to understand. You see, there are so many stages to making that kind of statue you see in Trafalgar Square or in Times Square if you like. If I may just explain, as I was saying to that lady . . .

KAMINI. You are telling me I can't understand? You tell His Excellency, Field-Marshal El-Haji Dr Kamini he can't understand! You telling me I stupid.

SCULPTOR. Mr President, I swear, I did not mean any such thing. As God is my witness, if I can just explain . . .

KAMINI. You say I cannot understand. That means you call me stupid! Me, you common Makongo carver, you call head of state a stupid man. In Bugara own embassy. On Bugara sovereign territory!

SCULPTOR (*resigned*). Well, Your Excellency, I cannot deny that charge more than I have already. I very humbly apologise, sir. You have taken the wrong meaning, I swear to that. It could happen to anyone. You are more powerful than me, I know you can report me and get me sacked . . .

KAMINI. Report you? Report you? To whom, you Makongo carver?

SCULPTOR. To my bosses in London of course.

KAMINI (*breaks into a loud guffaw*). Report you to your
bosses? What for? I may as well report you to the Secretary-
General of the United Nations. Ho, listen my friend, because
I like you so much, I tell you of project. Sit, sit . . .

SCULPTOR. Actually, if you don't mind, sir, I'd rather remain
standing.

KAMINI (*bellows*). I said SIT!!!

Hurriedly, the SCULPTOR *uncovers one of the chairs and
sits.* KAMINI *remains standing, staring at him.*

So? And where you want me to sit?

The SCULPTOR *leaps up again, looks round the room at
the several chairs, finally up the stairs towards the three
heavy armchairs.*

SCULPTOR. Do you want me to bring one of those Your
Excellency?

KAMINI. Ha, so you remember I am His Excellency. Good. It
is good you sit in same chair as Excellency? That makes sense
of protocol to you? If your people have no culture, we have.

KAMINI *watches the* SCULPTOR's *confusion for a while,
then takes the chair the* SCULPTOR *was about to use, and
points to the floor. The* SCULPTOR *quickly squats down.*
KAMINI *beams broadly.*

Now my friend, is that not looking better? In our country
a young man never sits on same level as his elder. If you
coming to Bugara, maybe marry Bugara girl, is good you
learn something of Bugara culture, not so? (*He looks round.*)
Maybe is even better I find seat much much higher than this.
After all, you common Makongo carver while Field-Marshal
El-Haji Dr Kamini full Life President of soveriegn state. (*He
begins to climb the stairs.*) Also, I have unfinished business
so to speak. Must try to kill two birds with one stone as you
say in Queen Elizabeth English, not so? I like Queen
Elizabeth, the royal family is my very good friend. Is why I
like Gudrum. She remind me something like the Queen
Mother.

KAMINI *has taken off his jacket. He lays it very carefully over the back of his chair. He unbuckles his belt and moves towards the toilet door. When he gets to the door he gestures to the* TASK FORCE SPECIAL *who emerges, dragging his* PRISONER, *his head dripping wet and spluttering.*

KAMINI. You wait outside till I finish private business.

KAMINI *is seen lowering his trousers, then his bulk onto the toilet seat, remaining visible from the waist up through the door. He raises his voice.*

KAMINI. Hey my friend, white Makongo carver, you still hearing me?

SCULPTOR (*his gaze rivetted on the dripping* CHAIRMAN, *he swallows hard*). Yes, Your Excellency.

KAMINI. Good. Because I want to tell you of project which I make from your carving. I am looking at this statue and I think, is time to make new Bugara currency. Same thing as I beginning to tell my chairman of Bugara Bank but instead he prefer to insult our sovereign currency. So, as I am thinking, is time to change the picture on our currency and I am thinking I use photo of that statue for the currency. What you think of that eh?

SCULPTOR. I think it's a very good idea Your Excellency.

KAMINI. You think is good idea enh? Better Kamini statue be on face of currency than sit in Madame Tussaud Chamber of Horrors, is that what you say?

SCULPTOR (*clutches his head*). Christ! She told him! The bitch! She went and told him.

KAMINI. What you say my friend? You think Kamini belong in Chamber of Horrors, not so? Not very good thing to say about Life President the Field-Marshal El-Haji, Dr Kamini, DSO, VC LD, PhD, DSc and so on and so forth from universities all over the world. But I like you. Perhaps some day I visit you in Queen Elizabeth England. You show me round London, take me to Madame Tussaud waxwork exhibition and we see Chamber of Horrors where you say Kamini belong. What you say about that my friend?

The SCULPTOR *looks round wildly, trapped. He half-rises, as if thinking of flight, looks up to see the* TASK FORCE SPECIAL *watching him closely, and changes his mind. The door opens diffidently and the* AMBASSADOR *enters. She takes a look at the* SCULPTOR, *then upwards at the* TASK FORCE SPECIAL *on the balcony.*

AMBASSADOR. Have you seen His Excellency? I can't find him anywhere.

KAMINI. Who's that?

AMBASSADOR. It's me, Your Excellency. I have been looking everywhere for you, Your Excellency. Your guests are waiting to . . .

KAMINI. You! If you are not careful I dismiss you. I am looking everywhere for you and you tell me now you are looking for me. Where you go all this time? Why you are not looking after my brother Excellencies?

AMBASSADOR. Your Excellency, I was on the phone talking to the Secretary-General. He called on the emergency number over the matter of Your Excellencies' statues.

KAMINI. I have no emergency when it is my lunch time, how many times I tell you that?

AMBASSADOR. But I know that, Your Excellency. That is why I undertook to discuss the matter with him myself. He has been in contact with the Russians and the Americans over the proposal.

KAMINI. Good. The Secretary-General is a civil servant, that is all. I should be calling him, not that he should call me. Next time he wants to call, tell him he must make an appointment.

AMBASSADOR. I will Your Excellency.

KAMINI *rises, pulling his trousers up, and emerges fully, zipping up and adjusting his belt.*

KAMINI. Is best I can do now but maybe I have more for you when I have finished lunch. (*He jerks his head towards the toilet. The* CHAIRMAN, *horrified, is prevented from flinging himself at* KAMINI's *feet and is frog-marched into the toilet, blubbering.*)

KAMINI (*to the* AMBASSADOR). What you doing there waiting?
Go and tell my brother Excellencies I coming now. Serve
them drinks.

AMBASSADOR. They've been served Your Excellency. I shall
inform them you are on your way. (*She goes.*)

KAMINI *carefully puts on his jacket, adjusts his medals and
descends the stairs.*

KAMINI (*standing over the* SCULPTOR). So you don't know
even to stand up when head of state enter in room. Is that
how you do when Queen Elizabeth or Richard Nixon enter
room in England or America?

SCULPTOR (*scrambles up, confused and scared*). I am sorry
Your Excellency, very sorry. I just didn't know whether . . .
I mean you yourself ordered me to sit down Your
Excellency.

KAMINI. Still no get sense, you white Makongo carver. No get
sense at all. (*He goes.*)

The SCULPTOR *stands still for some moments. He looks up
in the direction of the toilet from which very strange sounds
are coming. He walks back to the statues and completes the
task of covering them up in plastic sheets. He exits slowly.
He is hardly half out through the door when his body is
forcefully propelled from outside. His muffled scream is
followed by blows and the sound of stamping boots. Further
groans and blows, then the sound of a body being dragged
along the ground. Upstairs, the toilet is flushed.*

PART TWO

Voices coming in from outside. Enter a GUARD who carries in another chair which is brother to those already on the top landing. He climbs the stairs and rearranges the others to make space for the fourth. KAMINI enters, followed by his three brother HEADS OF STATE and the SECRETARY-GENERAL. KAMINI speaks as he leads the way up the stairs, begins to fiddle with the chairs for a more satisfactory arrangement, positioning the other three crowned heads, changing his mind, then trying something else. The SECRETARY-GENERAL remains at the foot of the stairs. KAMINI shows all the signs of having dined well; picking his teeth and belching from time to time.

SECRETARY-GENERAL. It's all a great pity Your Excellency. I don't quite know what we can do about it.

KAMINI. You are a clever man Mr Secretary-General. If you are not, we will not make you Secretary-General. You solve big problems. I not see why you cannot solve simple matter of culture. (*Turning to the others.*) Is matter of culture, not so?

KASCO. *Ah, oui. Evidement.*

GUNEMA. *Si si, verdaderamente.*

KAMINI. Or maybe you send for UNESCO of Paris to solve the matter.

SECRETARY-GENERAL. I don't think that will be necessary Mr President.

KAMINI. Perhaps is because you have not had your lunch? Why you not let my ambassador give you quick snack of lunch? You know, sometimes big problems which seem BIG, BIG, they disappear like that when I have eaten good dinner. Is true the brain is here (*He taps his head*.) but, as we say in Bugara, sometimes, when a man is body tired, the brain fall down (*He pats his stomach*.) — here. (*He guffaws, joined by all three*.)

SECRETARY-GENERAL. Well, I am glad Your Excellency is in such excellent spirits. We also have a saying in Bogota, 'Laughter is the tequila which corrodes the machete of anger.' I take it Your Excellency is no longer angry — no, in fact that is too strong a word — let us say, no longer disappointed with the United Nations.

KAMINI *has stopped fiddling with the chairs. He gives the* SECRETARY-GENERAL *a long studied look*.

KAMINI. You have proverbs in your country too?

SECRETARY-GENERAL. You forget Mr President, we are also a Third World country. We have many meeting-points in our cultures.

KAMINI. Hn-hm. Then I tell you another lesson of our culture. Do you notice what time you arrive at our embassy?

SECRETARY-GENERAL (*puzzled*). No, I did not particularly notice the time.

KAMINI. No, think. Try and remember when ambassador bring you in, what do you find me and my President brothers doing?

SECRETARY-GENERAL. Well, I think you had just finished lunch. Yes, you were just rising from the table.

KAMINI. There you are. In Bugara, a man who come to your house unexpectedly when you are just beginning or in middle of meal, with your family or your friends, that man is a good friend. He means well with you. But the man who arrive when you have finished, when the pots have been emptied and you are picking your teeth, that man is to be watched. It means the man has done something bad to you or will do so before the end of the day.

KASCO. *Ah oui? Chez nous aussi!*

GUNEMA (*nodding*). El Colonel Aranja, my late *capitan* of the

Palace Brigade of Guards, it happen like that with him. One day he come my house as my family finish . . . yes, I remember, we eat paella that afternoon. We finish eating, he enter the dining-room unceremoniously, over urgent matter. We talk, I watch him. That very night, I dream he plan coup d'etat against me. I arrest him in the morning and the tribunal find him guilty. I give him firing squad.

SECRETARY-GENERAL. Your Excellencies, I can see that you've all had a good lunch. Shall we just agree then that this has been just a misunderstanding? I promise I shall look for a solution.

KAMINI. But when, Mr Top Civil Servant?

SECRETARY-GENERAL. Naturally in due course Your Excellencies. Nothing can be done during this present session.

GUNEMA. *Caramba!*

KAMINI. My people will be disappointed. The black peoples will be disappointed all over the world, and especially in this country. The whole of the Third World will be disappointed. My ambassador has already make press release, all the television networks have been invited to make record of the historic day. How can you do this thing when we were only helping you in your work to make United Nations better?

SECRETARY-GENERAL (*in despair*). Helping me! (*As he turns round in despair, he sees for the first time, the covered group of statues. Eyes popping, he turns back slowly to* KAMINI *and Co*.) Dr President Kamini, is this the thing you propose we put up in the Delegates' Passage of the United Nations?

KAMINI. Is not finished. My Life President General Tuboum has just arrived and now he is to join the group.

SECRETARY-GENERAL. When the ambassador spoke to me about statues, I somehow thought she meant statuettes.

GUNEMA. Statuettes? What that?

SECRETARY-GENERAL. Small statues — (*Indicating*.) Like that. The kind of small busts which are made in factories. For distribution.

KAMINI. Small busts?

SECRETARY-GENERAL. Like the bust of Beethoven. Or Shakespeare. Or Lenin. The kind you place on book shelves.

KAMINI. Small bust is not dignified for big place like United Nations. Later, I make small bust copies to distribute to all my people and sell internationally. Maybe that bring some foreign exchange to Bugara.

SECRETARY-GENERAL. Oh my God! Mr President, sir . . .

KAMINI. Dr Life President.

SECRETARY-GENERAL. Excuse me, Dr Life President, let us go back a little.

KAMINI. Yes, good idea. It was your idea in the first place, you agree? You make request of all nations.

SECRETARY-GENERAL. For the international gallery Dr President, for the United Nations international gallery. I invited all permanent delegations to bring with them one work of art representative of their culture, one work of art only, to be exhibited in the international gallery.

KAMINI. So why now you making problem? Our three brother countries . . .

TUBOUM. Four.

KAMINI. I am sorry, now four. Four of our countries have come together to present your United Nations with one work of art. What now your problem Mr Secretary-General?

SECRETARY-GENERAL (*exasperated*). Have you seen the size of the International Gallery Dr President?

KAMINI. My ambassador see it, that is why she recommend different place. Top of stair. Delegates Passage. We are all agree.

TUBOUM. I was not consulted, but I am in full agreement with the wishes of my brothers. It is your duty, Mr Secretary-General, to bow to the wishes of our collective voice. We are firmly together in this.

SECRETARY-GENERAL. Your Excellencies, I do not

understand why you have set out to embarrass my
Secretariat in this way.

KASCO (*fuming*). Embarrass? *Mon Dieu*, embarrass? Who is
embarrass? Who is create the embarrassment? Is better for —
one, two, three, four heads of states to be embarrassed or for
one *functionaire*, *oui*, even if *haut functionaire*, to be
embarrass? You wish to embarrass me, *mon ami*, and that is
NOT HAPPEN — *non, jamais!*

TUBOUM. I mean, what do we tell the world Press? It is
intolerable.

GUNEMA. We do not permit, no.

KASCO. *C'est de la lèse majesté, n'est pas?*

KAMINI. I think now we resume sitting. Give time for sculptor
to finish work. (*He presses the bell.*) You spend too much
time talking Mr Secretary-General. Time you go back and
start finding solution to simple matter.

Enter the AMBASSADOR.

AMBASSADOR. Dr President?

KAMINI. Tell the artist man we are ready for him.

AMBASSADOR. Yes, Dr President. And er, Professor Batey is
here, Dr President. He has brought a revised draft of your
speech with him. Would you like him to come in and give
you a summary?

KAMINI. Good man, my friend Professor Batey. Tell him to
come in. He read the whole speech to us while we sit for
that artist man to finish his work. My brothers, you will give
me your opinion of the speech, I beg you.

Exit the AMBASSADOR.

TUBOUM. My pleasure.

KAMINI. Mr Secretary-General, perhaps you like to hear speech
too, then you contribute your opinion? But you must
promise not to steal Kamini's ideas for your own. Too much
of this stealing of idea in United Nations. Not good for
world peace.

An armed GUARD *enters, holds the door open for the*
SCULPTOR. *He is swathed in bandages from head to toe.*
Only his arms appear uninjured. His eyes barely peep out
through a mummified face. The SECRETARY-GENERAL
stares.

SECRETARY-GENERAL. What on earth happened to him?

KAMINI. Oh him? I know he look like something from
Chamber of Horrors. (*Convulses with laughter.*) He fall off
ladder I think. Not serious accident. We take good care
of him. Well Mr Secretary-General, I expect you to settle
everything at the United Nations.

On hearing the words 'Secretary-General', the SCULPTOR
raises his head, stares hard and limps as fast as he can towards
him. He tries to speak through the bandages but only
muffled sounds emerge. In desperation he attempts to tear
off the bandages.

Stop that bloody man!

The GUARD *rushes forward and pinions the* SCULPTOR's
arms behind him, making him wince in pain. KAMINI *then*
stomps down the stairs, his face contorted in fury. As he
faces his victim however, his manner suddenly changes, and
he breaks into a big, paternal grin. He wags a playful finger
at the man.

KAMINI. You are a bad boy, a very naughty boy. You know
the doctor say you must leave the bandages on for rest of
week. How else you going to get healed if you continue to
remove dressing. We take good care of you after your
accident. But if you continue to tamper with dressing, what
happen? The wounds become infected. Perhaps your leg get
gangrene and then the doctor must do amputation. Perhaps
even your head get infection and gangrene and then the
doctor must do amputation. You want Bugara embassy to
get blame I do not take good care of you? You will make me
angry if you try that again. Even Egyptian mummy get more
sense.

A bewildered SECRETARY-GENERAL *looks from the*

injured man to KAMINI *and back again, completely at a loss.*

SECRETARY-GENERAL. You are sure he should be working? Perhaps he should be in hospital.

KAMINI (*taking his arm and piloting him to the door*). He is very conscientious artist. Want to finish work in record time then go back to England, to his wife and children. He is my friend, he likes his work too much, like Makongo carver. (*To the* GUARD.) See that the Secretary-General is escorted to the gates.

Ignoring the SCULPTOR *completely as he walks past him,* KAMINI *resumes his place at the top of the stairs to encounter the questioning stares of his companions. The* SCULPTOR *shuffles back to his work.*

KASCO. *Mais qu'est-ce qu'il arrive?*

KAMINI. He is a very bad man. A spy. I think that Madame Tussaud Museum of England one big spy organisation, perhaps branch of MI5 of British Intelligence with support of CIA. My guards catch him climbing a window with a ladder. When they challenge him, he fall down from ladder.

TUBOUM. You should have shot him immediately.

GUNEMA. *Hijo de puta!* It is an international outrage. Expose him. Call press conference!

TUBOUM. What for? Everything will be denied. He will be disowned. You should shoot him and fling his body in the streets.

KAMINI. Perhaps I will shoot him. (*Looking pointedly at the* SCULPTOR.) It will depend on whether or not he finish sculpture in time for unveiling in UN. Then perhaps we give him reprieve.

GUNEMA. *Si, si.*

KAMINI. We have to teach all these super-powers that they cannot be sending their spies to be committing espionage with impunity. This is Bugaran Sovereign soil. I will not allow foreign spies to get away scot-free. They will be tried and punished under Bugaran laws because we are on Bugaran Sovereign territory.

KASCO. *Bravo mon frère, bravo!*

KAMINI. You do good statue, and you do it in time, perhaps I exercise good old Bugara clemency for you. If not . . .

The AMBASSADOR *ushers in* PROFESSOR BATEY *with papers.*

BATEY. Your Excellency, Dr Life President.

KAMINI. My good friend Professor Batey, you are welcome once again. And by the way, from now on, even if I am not here, this embassy is your own home. You must use it as if it is your own home. Madame Ambassador, I hope you are taking good notice. I want Professor Batey to have everything he wants anytime day and night.

AMBASSADOR. Yes, Your Excellency. (*The* AMBASSADOR *leaves.*)

BATEY. You are very kind Your Excellency. (*He glances curiously at the* SCULPTOR, *hesitates and appears to wait for instructions.*)

KAMINI. Well, read on, Professor Batey. I want to hear my speech, how it sounds. My brothers will tell me whether I will make impressive speech.

BATEY. Of course Your Excellency. But er . . . (*He glances pointedly at the* SCULPTOR.)

KAMINI. Oh him, he is just common spy but he good Makongo carver now. Like good brass monkey, he hear nothing, he see nothing and he speak nothing. You read out my speech, perhaps he learn plenty from it.

BATEY. Very well Your Excellency. I have er . . . tried to touch on the general world situation, especially the trouble spots and the position of the Third World vis-à-vis such crisis-torn spots. I remembered from our last discussions in Bugara, Your Excellency, that your burning concern above everything else is the total liberation of apartheid South Africa.

KAMINI. Oh yes. You still remember the famous air, land and sea military exercise I make to demonstrate how I will

defeat South Africa. I invite all the embassies. It was serious
mock battle I tell you. It make Vorster shit in his pants.

BATEY. It was a memorable event Your Excellency. Not only
impressive but moving. The commitment behind it all, it was
most inspiring.

KAMINI. Yes, yes. But read on, professor. Read me the whole
speech. My brothers want to hear how it sound.

BATEY. Of course Your Excellency. (*He clears his throat.*)
Mr Chairman, my brother and sister heads of state
honourable delegates to the United Nations . . .

The AMBASSADOR *re-enters. She coughs to attract
attention.*

KAMINI. What is the matter? Why you come here to disturb my
speech?

AMBASSADOR. I apologise Your Excellency, but we seem to
have an emergency. Two members of the Russian delegation
have just called. It would seem that the Secretary-General
tried to get them to approve the installation of Your
Excellencies' statues in the UN and has met with some
difficulties. Finally they insisted on coming to see the work
of art itself before coming to a decision.

KAMINI. Very careful people, the Russians. But they are my
friends, I know they will support me. Bring them in, bring
them in. And get ready to give them lunch.

The AMBASSADOR *goes out.*

GUNEMA. I approve the Russians. But they try to make trouble
for my small country.

TUBOUM. All the big powers make trouble. Only the Chinese
are different. They come, help to build our railways and
factories. They bring their own food and they never make
trouble.

KAMINI. The Chinese are my friends. But they have no money.

KASCO. I say any day — *Vive la France!*

BATEY. What of America, Your Excellencies? You all say

nothing of the good old US of A.

KAMINI. Oh we discuss America when we eat lunch, and it give us indigestion.

Enter TWO RUSSIANS. *They see the statue almost as soon as they enter, and it stops them dead.* KAMINI *and the others watch them. The* RUSSIANS *then turn slowly and fix their gazes on the four figures above.*

1ST RUSSIAN (*speaking in Russian*). Fraternal greetings of the government of the Union of Soviet Republics to illustrious leaders of the African continent.

2ND RUSSIAN. The leader of our delegation brings with them the fraternal greetings of the government of the Union of Soviet Republics and its peoples and declare ourselves greatly honoured to be in the presence of no less than four of the most illustrious leaders of the African continent.

1ST RUSSIAN (*speaking in Russian*). We are particularly revolted by the unexpected presence of the General Barra Boum Boum Tuboum, the well-known neo-colonial stooge and shameless exploiter of his own African peoples.

2ND RUSSIAN. Comrade Rostovich especially felicitates Life General Barra Boum Boum Tuboum for his courageous defeat of the imperialist conspiracy launched against him in his country by neo-colonial stooges and agents who are attempting to instal puppet regimes all over the continent in order to facilitate their shameless plans for the continuous exploitation of the struggling peoples of Africa.

TUBOUM. You see. I told you. They already know the name which my own people give me after I crush the dirty plotters.

KAMINI. They are our friends. I like the Russians. Please . . .

1ST RUSSIAN (*speaking in Russian*). How the spirits of the great Lumumba, Nkrumah, and even Jomo Kenyatta must be squirming in their graves.

2ND RUSSIAN. It is our great consolation that despite the machinations of the Western world in various guises, the spirit of Lumumba, Jomo Kenyatta, Nkrumah and other great heroes of the African liberation struggle lives on for ever.

PROFESSOR BATEY *appears to have become agitated. He makes as if to speak, changes his mind and begins instead to take notes.*

1ST RUSSIAN (*speaking in Russian*). However, let's get to the business of the international gallery.

2ND RUSSIAN. Now, regarding this proposed contribution to the United Nations International Gallery . . .

KAMINI. Yes, yes, what you say? You see it there before you. Good work of carving, not so. It remain just one more figure and the artist promise to finish tomorrow . . .

2ND RUSSIAN. Yes, Your Excellency. The comrade leader of our delegation was saying that the Secretary-General has discussed the matter fully with us. Our position will now be stated.

1ST RUSSIAN (*speaking in Russian*). Ask the buffoon if he really thinks he deserves an honour which is yet to be bestowed on our own national hero, Vladimir Ilyich Lenin.

2ND RUSSIAN. While we have no objection whatever in principle, our delegation feels that, in order that the United Nations does not appear guilty of discrimination in reverse, the statue of our great genius, the builder of modern Soviet Union Vladimir Ilyich Lenin must first be found an appropriate place of honour in the United Nations building.

1ST RUSSIAN (*speaking in Russian*). OK, enough of the charade. Give him the Babushka doll.

2ND RUSSIAN. We have therefore withdrawn the Babushka doll which was our original contribution to the Gallery of International Arts and Crafts and propose to substitute in its place a life-size statue of our beloved and revered Ilyich.

1ST RUSSIAN (*speaking in Russian*). Tell the overgrown child to enjoy himself tearing off the Babushka's limbs instead of those hapless Bugaran workers and peasants.

2ND RUSSIAN (*opening his briefcase and bringing out a doll*).

In the confidence that you will in turn support our proposal, and as a souvenir of yet another example of mutual cooperation, may we have the honour of presenting you with the Babushka doll which was our original contribution to the gallery.

KAMINI *rises to his fullest height and begins to descend the stairs, beaming broadly.*

KAMINI. My good friends, of course you have my support. And when I return to Bugara and tell my people how you have helped me against that civil servant who was trying to be so troublesome . . .

KAMINI *has stretched out his hand to take the doll when* BATEY *suddenly strides forward and knocks it off the* RUSSIAN's *hand. Consternation all round.*

KAMINI. What mean this Professor Batey?

BATEY. I speak Russian, Your Excellency. Ask them what they really said. I wrote some of it down — here.

He hands over the notebook to KAMINI. *The* RUSSIANS *exchange furious Russian with* BATEY.

KAMINI (*looking from the notebook to the* RUSSIANS *in mounting fury*). Ha! So, Kamini has mind of a child. Is that what you say? I, Kamini, I have mind of a child and you want to humour me? Thank you very much, thank you very much, thank you very much indeed. I am very humoured. I am laughing, do you see, I am laughing to death. (*Turning to the stairs.*) My brothers, you see? They call Kamini butcher. They say me I am butcher, a buffoon. They say I am reactionary bastard, killing and torturing my own people. They say while my people are starving to death in Bugara I am trying to impose my statue on the United Nations. Over their dead body they say. Look, I show you. (*He bounds up the stairs, thrusts the notebook at the others and turns round to face the* RUSSIANS.*) So I am not fit to wipe the dust of Lumumba's shoes, that is what you think. You say I think myself another Nkrumah or Lumumba but that everyone knows I am . . . what that word again? (*He snatches the* *notebook*.) Yes, I am — cretin? Professor, what mean cretin?

BATEY. You must excuse me Your Excellency. Anything you like, but don't ask me to soil my mouth with their disgusting slander.

KAMINI. It does not matter. You call me a vicious child, then you give me Babushka doll to play with. I, Life President Dr El-Hajj Kamini, DSO, VC, PhD, LLD many times over, you give me Russian doll to play with! You insult me and you insult my people.

The RUSSIANS *continue to protest but their protestations are mostly drowned by* KAMINI'*s mounting fury.*

2ND RUSSIAN. Your Excellency, it is a lie. This man must be an agent of the US government. This is the typical trick played by the United States government to ruin the cordial relationship between the progressive governments and our brothers in the Third World.

BATEY. How dare you! I detest the US government and what it is doing to our black brothers everywhere. My credentials are impeccable.

2ND RUSSIAN. Oh yes. CIA credentials. No doubt they are impeccable.

BATEY. You cannot twist your way out of this.

1ST RUSSIAN (*speaking in Russian*). Remind His Excellency of our constant support for him in the United Nations.

2ND RUSSIAN. Your Excellency, ask yourself. If what this fiction says is true, why do you think our government has given you so much support? No other government has defended you so stoutly against the slander of the Western Press. On the forum of the United Nations our delegation, led personally by Comrade Rostovich here, has constantly voted against and helped to defeat the libellous motions brought against your government by the imperialist regimes. We have defeated all the calls for a commission of enquiry into allegations of genocide and so-called violations of human rights. Human rights! We denounced them all as hypocritical cant, which is all they are. Mr President . . .

KAMINI. Dr President.

2ND RUSSIAN. Dr President, ask yourself the question. Try and resolve the contradiction if you like.

BATEY. You are very glib, but it won't work.

2ND RUSSIAN. Your Excellency, when the US and the United Kingdom removed their military experts, we stepped in and re-armed your armed forces. We provided you MIGS and trained your pilots. Who stepped in to train your Security Forces, enabling you to defeat coup after coup attempt? Our ambassador in Bugara personally exposed to you three attempted coups. Thanks to our information you were able to purge your army of traitors and their quisling collaborators right inside your cabinet. This is nothing but a shabby plot Your Excellency. We are astonished and offended that you should take it seriously for even one second.

KAMINI *appears to have begun wavering. He eyes* PROFESSOR BATEY *ominously.* BATEY *quietly reaches in his breast-pocket and brings out a mini tape-recorder.*

BATEY. Your discussion. I have it all down on tape. We can call in an independent opinion.

2ND RUSSIAN. Ha! He moves about with a secret recorder. Who now says he is no CIA Agent?

BATEY. I always work with a tape-recorder. His Excellency invited me to assist him with his speech to the General Assembly. Naturally I sent for my tape-recorder. I switched it on when you went funny on him.

2ND RUSSIAN. Good. We call in an expert. Your Excellency, we ask you to take immediate possession of the tape so that this man cannot tamper with it. The CIA is ruthless in its operations. Good-day Your Excellencies.

KAMINI. Where you think you go?

2ND RUSSIAN. Back to our embassy Your Excellency. We will make an immediate report of this matter so that appropriate action can be taken against this latest outrage by the CIA.

KAMINI. No. Nobody go anywhere. First we send for independent expert who listen to tape and make translation. After that . . .

2ND RUSSIAN. I regret we cannot wait that long Dr President. We have other things to do in the meantime. If you would be kind enough to telephone the embassy after you have obtained an independent Russian linguist . . .

KAMINI. No, you not go anywhere. This matter come first.

2ND RUSSIAN (*after quickly conferring in a low voice*). I regret Dr President . . .

KAMINI. You regret only if you insist you go.

2ND RUSSIAN. Without meaning any disrespect Mr President . . .

KAMINI. Dr El-Haji Life President!

2ND RUSSIAN. Without any disrespect, Your Excellency, this is getting ridiculous.

KAMINI. Ridiculous? I am ridiculous you say?

2ND RUSSIAN. Not you, Mr President . . .

KAMINI. I, Dr El-Haji Field-Marshal . . .

2ND RUSSIAN. No one has suggested for a moment, Your Excellency, that you are ridiculous. I merely point out that this present situation is ridiculous. It is ridiculous because we are ready to return to our embassy this minute, this very second, and you say we cannot leave. It is ridiculous because that suggests that you wish to keep us here against our will.

KAMINI. What is ridiculous about that?

2ND RUSSIAN (*pause while he digests this*). You will keep us here by force?

KAMINI. I say you stay here until I bring expert. I say you stay and that means you stay. Enough of this foolishness. (*He reaches for the bell.*)

BATEY (*growing increasingly alarmed*). Your Excellency, if I may intervene, I er . . . I don't think it is wise to detain these diplomats against their will.

KAMINI. Why not? We want to make investigation. So, every-body wait until investigation completed. Plenty of food and drink in the embassy. We even have vodka. But no caviar.

BATEY. Please Your Excellency, what I am trying to say is that it may lead to serious international repercussions. When they later complain that they have been detained against their will, I mean, the entire international community will be up in arms.

KAMINI. Why you want them to escape? You make the accusation.

BATEY. Your Excellency, I don't want them to escape or anything. The evidence is here. I merely want to expose the truth, but there is the question of diplomatic usage Your Excellency.

KAMINI. Then let them wait and hear the truth. All of us, everybody including my brothers here. We wait!

2ND RUSSIAN. This cannot go on. We insist that we take our leave.

BATEY. Do let them go Your Excellency. It's a question of international law . . .

KAMINI. International law! I know my international law as well as anybody, even professors. This is Bugaran territory. It is Bugara soil where our embassy is standing. That means everybody here subject to Bugara law. Everybody, including diplomats who abuse and insult Bugara Life President. Even if President of United States come here and abuse Bugaran hospitality, he is subject to Bugaran law. (*To his colleagues.*) Is that no so?

OTHERS (*dubiously*). *Si, si. Oui, oui.* But of course.

KAMINI (*he has been pressing furiously on the bell*). Where is that ambassador? Always she disappears when I am looking for her. Professor, please look for her in dining-room. Perhaps she stuffing her ears with food.

BATEY. Certainly, Your Excellency.

The door opens before BATEY *gets to it and a* GUARD *enters, a folded sheet of paper in his hand.*

KAMINI. You. Where is ambassador?

GUARD. She gave me this to bring in to you, Your Excellency.

KAMINI. Why she not bring it herself? She knows very well I like her to bring everything to me with her own hand. Where is the idiot? (*Descending.*)

GUARD. I don't know Your Excellency. She rushed in, gave this to me and instructed me to wait ten minutes before presenting it to Your Excellency.

KAMINI. Ten minutes? Why such foolish instructions?

GUARD. She said Your Excellency was having serious discussions with the Russian delegation and should not be interrupted for at least ten minutes.

KAMINI. All right, bring it. I cannot teach these women anything.

He takes the paper, which is a telex, and opens it. He reads. His face hardens as he looks up.

Cow! Female bastard! She tell you wait ten minutes? So she can empty all the money in the embassy and run away? Bastard cow, she want to desert what she think is sinking ship enh? I show her! Call out my Task Force guards and seal up the gates. Round up everybody. Anyone try to leave, shoot him. Nobody to leave this embassy. (*He screws up the telex and flings it on the floor.*) I show them. I show them nobody mess around with Life President Dr El-Hajj Field-Marshal Kamini. I take personal charge of embassy now. Sons of stinking imperialist rats, I show them! (*He storms out shouting.*) And keep everybody away from telephone. Anybody try to phone, shoot his mouth!

Several moments silence after KAMINI's *exit. The* CROWNED HEADS *exchange looks, then turn their gaze on the crumpled paper on the floor.*

KASCO. *Monsieur le professeur,* perhaps you will oblige by retrieving that communication and reading the contents to us.

BATEY (*approaches it gingerly, but picks it up and smoothes it out*). Oh my God. There has been a coup in Bugara!

BATEY *continues to stare straight ahead, anguish all over his face.*

(*With intensity.*) It is grossly unjust! (*He covers his face with his hands and turns away.*)

KASCO (*after an exchange of looks between all three*). Is it an epidemic beginning you imagine?

GUNEMA. How you mean?

KASCO. Look the situation. First Tuboum, now Kamini. Who next?

GUNEMA. You think perhaps there is coordination? Time of General Assembly, danger for all absent heads of state?

TUBOUM. Oh, I think it is just a coincidence. Coup attempts are as common as floods or drought on the continent.

KASCO. Still perhaps I give orders for some general arrests. *Il faut décourager les autres.*

GUNEMA. Me, I lock up all possibles before I leave the country. Plus their families in case of very bad suspicion.

KASCO. I send telex I think. Imitation is the ambition of weak minds. I have many in my empire.

BATEY (*sudden outburst*). You slave. You sacrifice. You devote your entire existence, day after day, hour after hour, with no rest, no let up, no distraction. From a hundred tribes, tongues, cultures, religions, animosities and suspicions, you weld a single, united people. Deprived, reviled, sabotaged and subverted by outside forces, from whose exploiting hands you have wrested your people, put an end to their centuries of domination, sometimes through force of arms, but always with your share of heroic encounters, imprisonments, tortures and deportations. Wars of liberation side by side with your peoples, often with the crudest weapons of resistance, against the most sophisticated and lethal weaponry from their diabolical factories. Every new nightmare of destruction, anti-personnel mines, cluster-

bombs, nausea-gas and a hundred other barbarisms of
chemical warfare. Still you resist, yielding no quarter, saying
only, no, singing rather, for our people sing out their souls in
adversity: this land is ours, we shall retrieve it. The wealth
is the people's, we shall restore it. And dignity, the dignity
that is born to every man, woman, and child, we shall
enshrine it. The invader is driven out, but is the battle over?
No. You discover that the greed is still in their eye and they
bring new, camouflaged weaponry to bear in wresting from
your hands the fruits of your people's labour. Eternally
vigilant, sifting through the deceptions of diplomacy and the
traps of proferred friendship, you ensure that the wolf of
yesterday does not parade before you as the sheep of today.
And sometimes even the people you serve must betray you;
that is the unkindest cut of all. Bought, or simply misguided,
blinded by their own greed or incapable of transcending
their petty clan loyalties, they desert the lofty heights of
your vision and burrow busily beneath the mountains of
your dreams. Do you think our experience is any different,
those of us from the mother continent who were settled here
as slaves? We had a man here, a king among men who once
declared, I have a dream. He revealed that he too had been
to the summit of the mountain of his dreams, your
mountain, the Kilimanjaro of every black man's
subconscious . . .

*Throughout his speech, the trio look at each other in
bewilderment. Finally*, KASCO *makes a move to stop him.*

KASCO. *Monsieur le professeur* . . .

BATEY. He was cut down by the bullets of an assassin.

KASCO. *Ah oui*, one must always safeguard the bullets.

BATEY. You don't understand. It was a conspiracy. And in
such another conspiracy, who do you imagine pulled the
trigger that felled Malcolm X. Who provided the guns?

KASCO. *Encore, oui Monsieur le professeur. Il faut toujours
sauvegarder les fusils.* You understand? It is an interesting
exposition and it make very interesting debate but right
now it is important I send instructions about guns to my

country. I must safeguard them from potential rebels. Please fetch me the *ambassadeur*.

TUBOUM. You forget. She has escaped.

KASCO. *Ah, oui.* And perhaps most of the embassy staff.

TUBOUM. Oh, you bet. By now the news must have spread.

GUNEMA. Rats! They desert the sinking ship. I despise them.

KASCO (*rises*). I have my aide-de-camp in the ante-room. Perhaps you will be kind to summon him, *Monsieur le professeur?*

BATEY (*unenthusiastically*). Certainly, Your Excellency. (*Under his breath.*) Pearls before swine. Saving their skin, that's all that matters now. (*As he passes by the* RUSSIANS, *he stops.*) And you are all the same. Cynics. You don't really care one way or the other do you?

2ND RUSSIAN. We are pragmatists. You should practise it sometimes.

BATEY. Pragmatists eh? I have another word for it but I won't bother you with it.

2ND RUSSIAN. Mr Professor, I am curious to hear what it is. Be assured, quite unlike your dethroned hero, we are not at all sensitive.

BATEY. I thought you could work it out yourselves — opportunists.

2ND RUSSIAN. Oh, is that all? I expected something worse. But really professor, to be practical now. As you see, the situation has changed. Field-Marshal Kamini has no further use for that tape, as you see. It is now a useless piece of potential embarrassment . . .

BATEY. You contradict yourself. If it is useless, then it has no potential for anything.

2ND RUSSIAN. I have no time to play with words, professor. Do let us have the tape. It is no longer of any value to Kamini whom it principally concerns.

BATEY (*studies them both for a while*). Isn't this interesting?

You sustain this man in power for years with the most
sophisticated weaponry. You train his secret service and
condone the so-called acts of suppression against his own
people. Yet in your heart of hearts, you despise him.

2ND RUSSIAN. Yes. A common butcher. We knew him. We
had close studies of him sent regularly by our own men, not
just Western reports. But in any case, we did not create
him — the British did. They sustained him in power, backed
by the Americans. Then they disagreed. The pupil had more
than mastered the game of his masters. So we stepped in
to fill the vacuum. I admitted to you Mr Professor, we are
pragmatists. Our policy in that part of the continent
required his retention in power. But you sir, what about
you?

BATEY. What about me?

2ND RUSSIAN. Come, come, professor, you are not naive. You
have visited Bugara. An intellectual, you have met many
Bugaran colleagues. Progressives, committed to the cause of
socialism — authentic socialism, not rhetorical. You have
spoken with them. Sometimes, surely you speak to them one
day, only to learn that they have disappeared the next? Their
bodies devoured by hyenas or floating down the Nile. Did
you really believe it was all Western propaganda?

BATEY. You claimed it was! You shouted it loud enough in the
United Nations.

2ND RUSSIAN. What was the word you used, professor?
Opportunism. It is our duty to discredit the Western press
when it tries to discredit the instrument of our policies. The
Western powers do the same — why not? But what about
you? You are here to write a speech for this er . . . heroic
leader. But what of the peasants and workers he has
destroyed at will? You write speeches on their behalf?

BATEY. He is a product of the economic and historical
conditions of our people on the continent. There is no such
thing as a monster — you, if nobody else, should be the first
to acknowledge that. You know it is colonial history which

must bear full responsibility for all seeming aberrations in
African leadership.

2ND RUSSIAN. I see. You have promoted these views among
the survivors of the Kamini's policies in Bugaran villages and
towns?

BATEY. No, I had no opportunity to . . .

2ND RUSSIAN. On your next visit perhaps. You see, professor,
we also believe that there are no eternal virtues. Like
honesty. It is a fiction. Or intellectual honesty, its later,
bourgeois refinement. Between our position and yours . . .
what shall we say? Please, the tape.

BATEY. I suppose you even had a hand in this coup? Maybe
that's why you took such relish in insulting him to his face.

2ND RUSSIAN. My government does not interfere in the
internal affairs of other nations. But — there appears to be
no longer reason for anything but frankness — you could say
that it became necessary to abandon him to his fate. His
presence in power no longer coincided with our interests.

KASCO. *Monsieur le professeur, je vous implore* . . .

BATEY. Forgive me Your Excellency, I'm on my way. (*To the*
RUSSIAN.) Put your minds at rest. I did take notes, but it
never occurred to me to switch on the tape recorder. There
is no recording. (*He goes.*)

KASCO *sinks back into his chair with a sigh, appears to shut
his eyes. The other two are equally busy with their own
thoughts. The* RUSSIANS *look at each other, come to a
decision. Opening the door slightly, one of them looks down
the passage, beckons to the other. They go. The* SCULPTOR
continues to work like a wraith.

KASCO. Ants, ants, what they understand? Gnawing away at
the seat of power. Flies, flies, what they care anyway?
Buzzing around the red meat of power. The red blood
attracts them, but what they do with the meat? Nothing.
They lay maggots, the meat fester. You shoo them away,
they run, buzzing away like noisy, excited children. What

they can do? Nothing. But you turn your back, they come
back — bz, bz, bz, bz. Power is the strong wind that drive
them away. When the wind fall, when the sail of power is no
longer fill, they come back. So, is better to squash them first
time. Don't blow them away, no. Squash them the first time,
then you are saved later trouble.

GUNEMA. Zombies. Turn them to zombies. Is better. Any fool
can understand government, but power! *Amigos,* that is
privilegio. To control the other man, or woman. Even for one
minute. Not many people understand that. When you control
from birth to death, when the other man and woman know,
in thousands or millions — I control your destiny from this
moment, from this consciousness till the end of your life,
now that is power. Even the animal world understand power,
even the insect world. I have studied the colonies of ants in
my garden. I sit down and meditate and collect my power
from the night, and I watch the insects. Is very useful.
I am not sentimental.

TUBOUM. I like to see the fear in the eye of other man. If he
my enemy, it is satisfactory. But it does not matter. If friend,
it is better still. Even total stranger. Because I see this man
telling himself, Tuboum does not know me, I am nothing to
him, so why should he do anything to harm me. But he is
afraid, I know it. I can see it in his eyes. I walk into a village,
nobody in this village has seen me before but, the moment I
arrive, I and my striped leopards — the village head, his wives,
the priest, the medicine man, they are afraid. Sometimes I
ask what is this fear I see? Have they been discussing treason
before my arrival? Have they been holding meetings with the
rebellious Shabira tribesmen? But I know this is not the case.
My spies have reported nothing, and they are good. They are
afraid, that's all. Barra Tuboum has brought fear into their
midst.

GUNEMA. I read once in a book — I think the author is Don
Guadajara — he write that power is an elixir. So I say to
myself, how I taste this elixir, how? That is when I go into
voodoo. With power of voodoo, I do many things, many
things impossible for ordinary man but still, I know I do not

taste this elixir. If I taste it, I know. I watch the execution of
these *mesquino* who think they want to take my power.
Firing squad, hanging, the garrot, but still I do not taste this
elixir. I do my own execution, take over gun, pull lever to
hang condemned man. I use the garrot myself but still, I do
not taste this elixir. I watch when my zombies torture lesser
zombies, I love their cries of pain, the terror before the pain
begins. With some I watch the strength become weakness like
baby, strong man cry like woman and beg to be put to death
instead of suffer. It give the sensation of power but still, I do
not *taste* this elixir.

KASCO. It is impossible, *mon ami*. You chase a will o' wisp.

GUNEMA. Ah, but it is possible. It happen finally, I tell you. It
happen like this. I sentence one man to death who I suspect
of plotting against me. While he is in condemned cell, his
wife come to plead for him. She is waiting all day in the
house and when I am going to dinner she rush through my
guards and fling herself at my legs, I am sorry for her. So, I
invite her to have dinner with my family. Well, I make long
story short. I tell her what her husband has done, that he is
an enemy of the state and that the tribunal is correct to
sentence him to death. She cried and cried, I feel sorry for
her but, justice is rigid span of power, it must not be bent.
My wife she is silent, she know she must not interfere in
affairs of state. That night, after my family retire, I take her
to bed. Perhaps she think by that I will reprieve her husband,
I do not know. We did not discuss it. But I take her hand,
and she follow me to my private bedroom. When I make love
to her, I taste it at last. It is a strong taste on my tongue,
my lips, my face, everywhere. It rush through my spine, soak
through my skin and I recognise it for that elusive, over-
whelming taste. Every night I made love to the woman, the
same taste is there, nothing to compare with it. Nothing.

KASCO. So you reprieved the husband?

GUNEMA. Oh no, that cannot be. He was hanged on the
appointed day. I pull lever myself. By then the woman had
become fond of me and we still meet and made love. But it

was gone. After the husband ceased to live, the taste vanished, never to return.

TUBOUM. I like the story. I like the story very much.

GUNEMA. It is true story, *amigo*.

KASCO. *C'est formidable. Formidable!*

TUBOUM. I like the story. So the woman remain your mistress. For long?

GUNEMA. Not for very long. After the taste was gone, I have to do something. I begin to fear she is plotting to take revenge for her husband's death. I ask, why does she still remain my mistress? I had her garotted. It was better. But it is a sad story, not so?

The door pushes violently open suddenly and the RUSSIANS *rush back inside, move to a corner and try to remain obscure. Moments later, two* US DELEGATES *are pushed in by armed* GUARDS. KAMINI *follows, also with a sub-machine gun levelled at the two captives. They are backed against the far wall.* BATEY *enters last, wearily.*

KAMINI. Yes, it is beginning to make sense. First, the World Bank refuse common loan. Then that Secretary-General! Kamini is never wrong. I know it from moment he arrive after we have finish eating, when we were picking our teeth and there is nothing left in the pot but bones. I said, yes, the vultures are gathering somewhere. There is something bad in the air, somebody is abusing Kamini or plotting bad for him. Now I know him plotting with World Bank. And to think I like that civil servant. I think always he is my friend.

US DELEGATE. But he is Your Excellency. We have come on the same mission.

KAMINI. Yes, do I not say it? Same mission. He come here, make espionage, the Russians follow, make espionage and insult Kamini to his face. I go out and I catch you sitting in my lobby with confidential embassy staff.

US DELEGATE. We had been waiting one hour Mr President. We were kept waiting one hour but we waited patiently for

Your Excellency to be done with the Russians. We came as soon as the Secretary-General raised the issue of the statues. We fully support the idea.

KAMINI. What statues? Oh yes, I forget all about statues. (*He goes off and appears to remain lost in thought for a while*.)

US DELEGATE. We did not want the Russians to claim credit for promoting the scheme. We rushed here as fast as we could but the Bolshies sneaked here ahead of us — as usual. Your ambassador refused to announce our presence, kept us in the lobby. What could we do? We waited patiently. Then everything started to go haywire. Your madame ambassador rushed in and out again like the embassy was on fire, then the guards came and rounded up everyone. We wanted to leave but were driven back at the point of guns, and then you came in, all armed . . . this is all highly undiplomatic usage Your Excellency. I suppose there must be an explanation.

KAMINI *is still lost in thought. The* US DELEGATES *look around in amazement at the presence of the other* CROWNED HEADS.

US DELEGATE. Good God. Everybody is here. What is going on anyway?

BATEY. Haven't you heard? There has been a coup?

US DELEGATE (*horrified*). Here? In the United States?

2ND RUSSIAN (*amused*). Oh. You think such a thing is possible in strong powerful democratic country?

US DELEGATE. Don't be so complacent. It will happen over in yours one of these days.

2ND RUSSIAN. Never!

US DELEGATE. You hope. So it's Bugara. When was this?

All eyes turn toward KAMINI.

KAMINI (*still half-absent*). Is great pity. Is pity I allow that top civil servant to escape. He cause the coup. It is a United Nations coup, sponsored by super-powers with World

Bank. Because Kamini is not slave. I say to British, bugger
off. I say to Americans, bugger off. Then the Russians came.
They think also they own Kamini. I tell them also, bugger
off. Now they make coup against me. All of them, join
together. They not fit to face Kamini, man to man one to
one inside Bugara, so they make coup from here with all the
United Nations super-powers. Is a pity I don't have their
stooge here, that top civil servant man whom I think my
friend. I know what I do to him, under Bugaran Law.

The two DELEGATES *exchange nervous looks.*

2ND RUSSIAN. Mr President sir . . .

KAMINI. Dr Life President!

2ND RUSSIAN. Dr Life President, I wish to assure you, at all
times . . .

KAMINI. Yes, always you assure Kamini. Always you assure
Life President of Bugara, but still, you stage coup. Your
KGB take care of my security, not so?

US DELEGATE. Perhaps I may come in, Field-Marshal Dr
El-Hajj. You need be in no fear that the US government will
recognise these rebels who have taken over — whoever they
are. As far as my delegation is concerned, the head of state
of Bugara is right here in this embassy standing before me.
My delegation will certainly insist that Your Excellency
address the Assembly tomorrow as planned and of course,
the proposal which we were bringing to Your Excellency
regarding your life-size statue, remains in force. We have
given it our unqualified support. The only condition we
attached to our support was that the statue of our own
nation-founder, George Washington be given appropriate . . .

KAMINI (*swinging the gun dangerously to and fro*). You hear?
Always they make condition. Everybody make condition.
Who get the idea in first place? Why then you bring me
condition? Is idea of Field-Marshal Dr Kamini, not so? You
bring condition because you don't want to see Kamini statue
standing in United Nations. While you come here talk
conditions, you plan coup. You telling World Bank, no loan

for Kamini. Is the fine trick of super-powers, we know. When you call conference and everybody is making talk at conference tables, you are undermining talk and giving weapon to all sides. When you are making disarmament talk, you are making more and more atom bomb. Why you not give me atom bomb when I ask you. Why not? Alright, answer me. I tell you, I want to destroy South Africa. South Africa is practising apartheid which is wrong. So I want to fight South Africa, but South Africa has atom bomb. I beg you for atom bomb, all of you. You smile. You think Kamini big fool . . .

2ND RUSSIAN. Be fair, Your Excellency. You wanted the atom bomb, not just for South Africa, but to use against your neighbour, the President of Hasena. And he is our friend. A good socialist friend. We were in a dilemma. You put us in a difficult position. Did we arm even our friend the President of Hasena with the atom bomb? Look at Cuba, another close friend of ours and yours, did we give them the atom bomb?

KAMINI. Is bad. Is very bad you don't give Cuba atom bomb. Cuba help us in Africa. Cuba is my friend. I like Cuba. I like Fidel Castro very much. He nice man. In fact, if Fidel Castro is a woman, I will marry him, but he must first shave off his beard. Why he wear beard like that? Make him look like guerilla. I don't like guerilla. They are bad *kondo* people, always creating trouble.

US DELEGATE. Precisely, Your Excellency. They foment trouble, aided and abetted by the Eastern powers, without any discrimination.

2ND RUSSIAN. And what of El Salvador enh? What of capitalist bandits in Nicaragua.

KAMINI. In my country, all so-called guerillas are bandits, armed robbers. When I catch them, I take them to their families. Or hang from tree. Only way to put a stop to that guerrilla syphilis imported from Western countries.

The RUSSIANS *smirk at the* AMERICANS.

TUBOUM. Camarade Field-Marshal, what is the plan?

KAMINI. Plan? What plan?

KASCO. *Oui, il faut prendre la decision.* What to do now? My
aide-de-camp, where is he? I must send message at once to
my head of security. A few heads perhaps must fall,
pour décourager les autres, you understand. Rebellion is
contagious disease, *n'est pas?*

KAMINI (*looks at him, surveys all the others*). Nobody going
anywhere. Not safe. I shall send for the Secretary-General.

Silent communication between the CROWNED HEADS.

TUBOUM. But my brother, when you say, nobody leaves,
surely, that cannot include our — entourage?

KAMINI'*s eyes shift nervously round.*

KAMINI. Nobody — leaves. If anybody leave now they make
propaganda. Tell lies that Kamini's brothers desert him in
trouble. Not good for us.

BATEY. Oh my God. My dear, respected, Field-Marshal
Dr President, if I may venture to advise. In such a crisis,
solidarity based on good will is absolutely essential.

KAMINI. Yes, solidarity. I believe in solidarity. My brothers,
they are with me. We make statue together for United
Nations. That is why nobody leaves.

A dull explosion is heard, close.

KASCO. *Au nom de Dieu!*

GUNEMA. What happen? We are under attack!

TUBOUM *has dived beneath the nearest chair. Footsteps
are heard racing towards the entrance. A* TASK FORCE
SPECIAL *enters, in suit.*

TF SPECIAL. Your Excellency, the strong room is now open.

KAMINI. Good work. That traitor, the ambassador, she take
the combination of the armoury with her, but we blow open
the door. Take out all the heavy artillery and position them
round the embassy. Two machine guns, grenade launcher and

a rocket launcher to be brought inside here. Booby-trap all doors and windows. Anyone break in, we blow the whole of Bugara sky-high. We are not fearing to die like men.

TF SPECIAL (*salutes*). Your Excellency, it will be done.

KAMINI. Wire the entire building. When Kamini says boom, let everything go boom!

TF SPECIAL. Understood Your Excellency.

The TF SPECIAL *goes. Alarm deepens all round, but is kept under control.* TUBOUM *re-emerges from cover.*

KAMINI. They will not dare attack this place. I have here both the leaders of the Russian and the American delegations. They will not dare attack.

US DELEGATE. My dear Excellency, I give you the word of the government of the United States, the grounds of every foreign embassy are sacrosanct. Of course no one would even dream of attacking. If such an unlikely aberration occurs, the United States will defend your sovereignty.

KAMINI. I have seen through your tricks. It is a plot of the United Nations. If the Russians agree on the hot line, you will allow Bugaran rebels to take over my headquarters. You agree everything between the two of you. You don't care about anybody else. Pity. If only your top civil servant is here.

Enter uniformed GUARDS *with machine guns and other weaponry.*|*The* TF SPECIAL *follows them.*

KAMINI (*indicating*). Machine gun on the balcony, by windows. Rocket launcher through that toilet door. The window overlook the park across to the United Nations. Anybody attack here, we reduce the United Nations to rubble, then blow up Bugara.

The rocket-launcher is taken upstairs. The hapless CHAIRMAN *is yanked out of the toilet to sprawl on the floor while the launcher takes his place.*

TF SPECIAL. I have to inform you, Your Excellency. The Secretary-General is at the gates, demanding to speak to you. I informed him of your strict instructions that no one was to enter or to go out . . .

KAMINI. The Secretary-General! Are you mad? Why you not escort him here immediately!

TF SPECIAL. Your Excellency, we merely carried out your instructions.

KAMINI. You son of a bastard, you are a traitor. Get him here or I finish you on the spot.

TF SPECIAL. I shall do so at once, Your Excellency.

KAMINI. Get out and see. (*The TF SPECIAL races for the door.*) And if he has gone, shoot yourself before you come back. (*He turns to the others in grim satisfaction.*) He come back henh? Now who can tell me this is not Bugara soil. The gods of Bugara bring him back to scene of his crime.

GUNEMA (*ingratiating*). *Amigo,* I do not wish to dispute the honour, but is Benefacio Gunema who bring him back, with voodoo. I think, if the *functionario* come back, then we your brothers can go. So, we go now I think, yes?

KAMINI. Is better all remain here — for your own safety. I know these people, you go out now, they do bad thing to you because they know you Kamini friend.

KASCO. *Mon Dieu,* we shall be the judge of that. It is important I make immediate contact with my imperial regent at home.

KAMINI. I tell you is not safe. By now anyway they have close all airports and cut off communications. I am sure they have set up roadblocks and shoot anybody on sight. But you are safe in Bugara. Field-Marshal El-Hajj Kamini personally guarantee your safety.

GUNEMA. Hey! *Es loco, no?* Crazy!

TUBOUM. S-sh! You know, I must congratulate you, comrade Field-Marshal. How did you manage to accumulate so much heavy weaponry here? I don't have anything like it in any of my embassies.

KAMINI. A-ha, you are forgetting that I am supporting all

revolutionaries everywhere. I put weapon in all my embassies so as to fight the imperialists. You ask, my diplomatic bag is always heavy.

TUBOUM. Admirable, truly admirable.

KASCO (*to* TUBOUM). *Il est dangereux, no?*

GUNEMA. *Muy loco, muy loco.*

Again TUBOUM *signals him not to speak so loud. The* SECRETARY-GENERAL *is ushered in.*

KAMINI (*swings the gun round to him*). So you come back, Mr Top Civil Servant. Welcome.

SECRETARY-GENERAL. I heard the news, Your Excellency. I felt I had to come personally and offer my sympathies. Also to ask what your plans are, if there is anything we can do while you are here . . . Your Excellency, I er . . . would you please point that thing away from me. I am not used to guns.

KAMINI. Sympathy? Perhaps you think Kamini simple child — after all you and these Russians the same, no? You plot together against me with the Americans.

SECRETARY-GENERAL. Your Excellency!

KAMINI. You make war against me, now I make war against you. You think Kamini finish? Ha ha! Kamini get big surprise for you. Now all of you, you move together in one place. You come to ask what you can do for me? I show you. Move. Over there.

He herds the SECRETARY-GENERAL *with the* RUSSIANS *and* AMERICANS *in a corner.*

SECRETARY-GENERAL. What is going on? This is preposterous.

2ND RUSSIAN. I think you do as he says.

US DELEGATE. I second that Mr Secretary-General.

KAMINI. You bet your life you do as Kamini say. Now you listen to me. I know there is no coup in the world which is not back by super-power. Ha. How I know? Of course the

British and American help me make my coup. I am living
witness. But I kick them out, they and their Zionists, and
then is Russia who is helping me all the time. Until they
refuse to give me atom bomb, and I am very angry with
them. I tell them to go back to Moscow. I lie? Your
government angry because I try to boot you out of Bugara.
Give you seventy-two hours to pack out your embassy bag
and baggage from Bugara.

2ND RUSSIAN. But that was a minor misunderstanding, Your
Excellency. It was all straightened out and you changed
your mind.

KAMINI. Changed my mind bloody hell. You changed
your mind. You plan coup but Kamini move fast. Round up
your stooges and shoot them. Take ring-leaders to their
villages and hang them there, then liquidate their regiment
in prison. So you had to change your mind and pretend
to settle quarrel. But you only wait new chance.

SECRETARY-GENERAL. If I may interrupt Your
Excellency, the whole world knows that the United Nations
never gets involved in the internal affairs of our member
countries.

KAMINI. You tell that to the marines, not to Kamini! What
Dag Hammarskjöld doing in Congo all that time Lumumba
killed? Not making coup? How he himself get killed if
not plotting all over the place and spying from aeroplane.
He too Secretary-General before you, not so? You all
pretend you are just civil servant but you take your nose
in matter which don't concern you. Why don't you go
upstairs Mr Secretary-General, see what you find pointing
from toilet window. Unless you do as I say, I begin to lobby
one rocket every five minutes to United Nations building.
As for you two super-powers, you send urgent message
to your governments, you tell them to undo their coup,
send International Force to Bugara to crush rebellion,
otherwise you don't get out of here alive. Nobody get out of
here alive. I have wired everywhere with bomb. You know I
always travel with my suicide squad and they have taken over

the embassy. You Mr Civil Servant, you will write to World Bank to bring Bugara loan here, in cash. Then write the General Assembly to pass motion condemning the coup. Get support of China — China too hate super-power game like me. I want United Nations recognise Kamini as President for Life. How can anybody topple Kamini when he Life President. Kamini alive and kicking. You send message to General Assembly or else I bring down that building to complete rubble.

BATEY (*approaching from behind*). In God's name Dr President . . .

KAMINI (*gives him a back-handed swipe that knocks him flat on his back*). You sneak up behind me again like that and you soon smell your mother's cunt. Get over there. You are CIA I think, to come behind a man like that. How I know you did not come to Bugara to spy for these super-powers. And then you come here today, like everybody. Everybody coming here today, coming here today. Why? Because you all coming to take over Bugara headquarters from me. But there you make mistake. Kamini good and ready for all of you. You never want black man to succeed, don't want his statue in United Nations, don't want him as Secretary-General, don't want him to become super-power and keeping the atom bomb to yourself . . .

Without, the noise of crowds beginning to gather. Occasional bullhorn order of 'move along there', 'keep to the pavement', 'other side of the road, please', etc. etc.

Who all these people?

TUBOUM. As far as I can make out, they appear to be demonstrators.

KAMINI (*big grin*). I knew it. My people have risen to defend the sovereignty of Bugara. (*To the* TF SPECIAL.) You, go and take a look and bring me report. (*The* TF SPECIAL *goes*.) Now we show them what is popular uprising. (*To the* US DELEGATES.) Perhaps you see revolution take place in your own super-power country. Yes? Is good for you. Perhaps

Bugara take over your capitalist country.

The chant however is clarifying into a chant of 'Out, out, out, Kamini, out, out, out, Kamini', interspersed with screams of 'assassin!'. 'butcher', 'cannibal', etc. etc. Sirens join in the commotion as police cars screech to a halt.

TF SPECIAL (*rushing in*). Bugaran refugees Your Excellency. They are carrying banners all over the place.

KAMINI. Nonsense. There are no refugees from Bugara. Is propaganda organised by imperialist countries.

TF SPECIAL. I saw some of the banners Your Excellency. One of them read 'BUGARAN EXILES FOR TOTAL LIBERATION.'

KAMINI. Shut up. Is a lie!

Sudden splinter of glass as a heavy object crashes through a window somewhere in the building.

They attacking already?

Another follows, and another. The next crashes through a window up in the balcony, narrowly missing the MACHINE GUNNER.

We are surrounded. (*He raises his voice and bellows.*) Fire!

SECRETARY-GENERAL. Your Excellency!

Instantly the guns pointing outwards from the balcony open up. KAMINI strides to the door, flings it open and bellows down the passage.

KAMINI. Fire! Shoot! Shoot!

Guns and rocket launchers open up everywhere. The whine of rockets mingles with the boom of exploding grenades. Screams and panic. The sound of the crowd in panicked retreat. Instinctively TUBOUM and KASCO have flung themselves flat. TUBOUM reaches up and pulls GUNEMA down with them, pulling out his gun. KAMINI swings back into the room, his gun aimed directly at the HOSTAGES. Their horror-stricken faces in various postures — freeze. The SCULPTOR works on in slow motion. Slow fade.